The Last Train Out

The Last Train Out

■ ■ ■

Rudy Seamayer

Transcribed and Edited by

Kay Lewis Seamayer

Copyright ©2015 Rudy Seamayer
All rights reserved.

ISBN: 151771544X
ISBN 13: 9781517715441

Dedication

To my wife and life partner, Kay: Thank you for loving and caring enough to bring my story, "The Last Train Out" to life.

I'm a lucky man to have three beautiful and devoted daughters; Ann, Karen and Erika who constantly fill my life with joy, fun and laughter. And to my three grands; Erika Laine, Alex and Nicholas, keep making your Poppy proud.

With infinite love, appreciation and gratitude, I thank everyone who helped me survive as a child during and after WWII; and to all those who were there in adulthood with a "hand up" to help me fulfill my life's dreams and goals.

Table of Contents

	Editor's Note	ix
	Introduction	xiii
Chapter 1	Early Childhood in a Changing World	1
	1930 – Werschetz, Yugoslavia	1
	A Day in the High Meadow with the Cows	3
	School Days	7
	Personal and Political Changes	8
Chapter 2	Escape on "The Last Train Out"	14
	Fall 1944	14
Chapter 3	From Werschetz to Germany	17
	October 1944	17
	Dangers Ahead	18
	The War Has Ended, But What Now?	27
Chapter 4	The Search for Family	32
	1945	32
	January 1946	34
	Tragedy Strikes Again	38
Chapter 5	Seeking Greener Grass on the Other Side	42
	Journey through School to Immigration	42
	1947 – Stuttgart, Germany	43

	College Graduation · · · · · · · · · · · · · · · · · 44
	June 1951 ·48
	One Bumpy Ride to Freedom and Opportunity ·50
Chapter 6	The American Dream · · · · · · · · · · · · · · · ·52
	Thanks be to God...We Made It! · · · · · · · ·52
	Welcome Home – to America · · · · · · · · · ·55
Chapter 7	The Soldier's Life in Germany · · · · · · · · · · · ·59
	1953 ·59
	"Hello, Aunt Tillie, It's Me, Rudi" · · · · · · · ·67
	Beautiful Vienna, Austria · · · · · · · · · · · · · ·76
	Farewell to Family · · · · · · · · · · · · · · · · · ·83
	Return to the USA · · · · · · · · · · · · · · · · · ·84
Chapter 8	At Home In America · · · · · · · · · · · · · · · · · ·86
	October 1955 ·86
	Surprises! Surprise! Surprise! · · · · · · · · · · ·97
Chapter 9	It's All About Timing · · · · · · · · · · · · · · · · · 102
	Chicago, June 1961 · · · · · · · · · · · · · · · · 102
Chapter 10	Return to My Homeland – 60 Years Later (Previously Werschetz, Banat Yugoslavia – Now Vrsac, Serbia) · · · · · · · · · · 120
	"Don't Go Back" · · · · · · · · · · · · · · · · · · 120
	Day Two in Werschetz · · · · · · · · · · · · · · 129
	Return from Hell · · · · · · · · · · · · · · · · · · 130

Editor's Note

■ ■ ■

FOR AS LONG AS I'VE known Rudy, (55+ years of marriage) family and friends have been fascinated with his unusual life story; his European history as a refugee and displaced person, his survival during and after WWII and his journey to citizenship and living the American Dream.

Basic reaction to his stories through the years has almost always the same: *You should write a book.* But Rudy, in his true character, never thought of his life story being any more fascinating or important than millions of others who survived the war with similar experiences of hardships and stories to tell. It's no surprise that our three daughters, Ann, Karen and Erika, and grandchildren, Erika Laine, Alex and Nicholas feel differently; for it is not only *his* personal life story, it's his heritage and legacy in which they all share.

I guess it would be safe to say I've heard these stories told a *few times* over the past fifty plus years. It was only after he returned from a visit to his homeland of Yugoslavia (now Serbia) sixty years after he fled, was he able to actually sit down with paper and pen and begin to unlock and relive those early childhood wartime experiences in more detail.

It's true, Rudy is a survivor of war, hunger and loss, but he has never considered himself a victim. His story is one of reality and acceptance of living life on its own terms; *and making it better.*

It's in this spirit of love, respect and purpose that I do my best to capture and share his life story with you in *The Last Train Out.*

Transcribed and Edited by Kay Lewis Seamayer

Kay Lewis Seamayer
October, 2015

Saint Gerard Twin Towers Catholic Church – Werschetz, Yugoslavia

Introduction

■ ■ ■

ARCHIVES IN THE SAINT GERARD Twin Tower Catholic Church in Werschetz, Yugoslavia, city of my birthplace (1930), trace the migration and settlement of "Family Seemayer" and countless others of Germanic descent back to the Habsburgs and Maria Teresa era of the 1700s.

There are several small countries and various ethnic groups who have lived and fought for political power and territory in this part of Europe ever since it was populated. Here is a brief overview of the complicated history of the area I'm referring to, which influences my story.

After decades of warfare between the Hapsburg Monarchy and the Ottoman Empire (Turks) in Eastern Europe in the 17th–18th centuries, the Turks were finally driven out, leaving the Danube Valley (belonging to Hungary at the time) virtually unpopulated. The Habsburgs began to repopulate the land with German settlers and various ethnic populations from the Austro-Hungarian Empire. Incentives offered to entice the Germans to resettle in Hungary included financial help for their long journey and a promise to allow them to keep their own language.

From the Swabian Black Forest region in Germany, settlers packed their personal belongings, tools, livestock and families onto wooden box type rafts and set sail on the Danube River, which flowed southeast all the way to the Black Sea. Once they reached Hungary along the Danube and located a suitable home site, they simply laid claim to the land by building homes using wood from the boats.

German migration to this region continued for some sixty years. As the population grew, churches were built, a governing body was formed and order was at hand. Although living conditions were harsh and resources were few, the Swabians continued to work hard, manage their assets and use whatever resources they had wisely in order to grow and flourish in the region.

Yugoslavia was created in 1918 after the collapse of the Hapsburg Austro-Hungarian Empire at the end of WWI, and it was formally named the Kingdom of Yugoslavia in 1929.

King Peter II was elected Monarch of Yugoslavia in 1928. During his democratic rule, life remained fairly stable during my early childhood until the Communist Party (influenced by Tito, who remained out of sight) took over in 1941. It was then German troops entered Yugoslavia, put the Communist Party in its place and returned relative calm and peace to the country. The German army remained there until 1944 when they were sent to other warring factions on the eastern front, leaving Yugoslavia vulnerable to Russian invasion.

That's when all our troubles really began. After all, anyone of German descent living in foreign lands (known as Volksdeutschers) was an automatic enemy of the Russians.

"Famalie Seemayer" Coat of Arms
An original woodcarving by Rudy Seamayer

CHAPTER 1

Early Childhood in a Changing World

■ ■ ■

1930 – Werschetz, Yugoslavia

I was born in an unusually peaceful time politically in Yugoslavia, to what might be considered a middle-class entrepreneurial family. My father, Julius, was a tailor, and my mother a homemaker with excellent skills and experience as a seamstress. They often worked together on specific projects. I guess I can say I helped too, as my dad often sent me to the sewing shop in town a few blocks away for thread and other items. He always gave me the same instructions:

"You run as fast as you can, and come right back."

"Yes sir, I'll be right back." I'd answer, although sometimes I got distracted by some of the Serbian kids always wanting to fight. It was not unusual for Serbian and German kids to get into street skirmishes. That's just the way things were at that time.

My sister Hildegard (we called her Hilde), eight years older than I, graduated from seamstress school and worked locally for a couple of years. In 1941, she moved to northern Germany to work.

Werschetz was the largest city in the region. By the early 1940s, the population was thirty-two thousand. Seventeen thousand were of German descent, with the remainder comprised of Serbians, Hungarians, Romanians, Turkish, White Russians and a few Gypsies. The Germans were industrious and hard working individuals and owned and controlled the majority of local businesses. They also had a very strong presence in city government.

Life was fun for us kids. We were very close to my mother's side of the family. She had one sister; Aunt Tillie and three brothers; Uncles Julius, Ferdinand and Ignatz. My cousins, Frank, Anne, Tilde, Ferdinand, Mitzi and Ignatz Jr. and I were very close. All three of my mother's brothers were wine farmers (grape growers) and owned their own small presses and wineries.

Werschetz was truly known as *wine country*. Most vineyards grew on mountain slopes. Work was strenuous for both workers and horses. After the grapes were cut, they were carried down the mountainside by workers wearing huge containers strapped to their backs. The grapes were then dumped into large barrels sitting on horse-drawn wagons. Each wagon usually transported two loads a day. When there was a bumper crop of grapes, some growers sold their excess loads to commercial distilleries and wine makers.

School let out for two weeks every fall to allow kids to help harvest grapes on their family farms. I looked forward to spending time with cousins every fall during grape harvest and on holidays.

In addition to growing grapes, my three uncles grew corn, wheat, hops and potatoes and raised their own horses, cows, chickens and pigs for their own use. Once a year in late fall, when the weather cooled down, my Uncle Julius butchered a large pig for our family in exchange for a new suit tailored by my father. It was a great celebration. All the family was invited to enjoy a fresh pork dinner followed by cards and other fun games. It was fun being a kid then.

In spring, the huge wine barrels standing as tall as the ceiling had to be cleaned inside. Wine stone built up over time and had to be chipped away about every third year. Entry into the barrels was very small (by design). I was the only one small enough to crawl inside. A candle was lit and placed inside the barrel. When the candle started to flicker, it was time to come out. So for a number of years, it was my job to chip away the wine stone. I can still recall the wonderful residual smell of that delicious freshly squeezed grape juice that went into those barrels.

A Day in the High Meadow with the Cows

One beautiful spring day when I was five years old, my next-door neighbor, Rudigard, and I were walking to kindergarten. In the distance, we heard the sound of cow bells. The sound comes closer and closer, and soon we're face to face with a whole herd of milk cows on their way to the meadow outside of town to graze on the fresh tender green grass.

Suddenly, I thought of a great idea.

"Hey, let's skip school today. We can follow the cows to the meadow then follow them back long before school is out. Our parents will never know we played hooky."

"Yeah, let's do it. No one will ever know," Rudigard replied.

The cows come closer. We step aside. As soon as the cows pass, we get in march step close behind them so the herder won't see us. The meadow seems a bit far, but we just keep walking. After all, the herder surely knew his way around.

Finally, we reach the high meadow. I wonder if the cows are as tired as we are. The herder doesn't seem to pay any attention to us as we skip rocks in the stream, dig up bugs from underneath rocks nearby and sit and amuse ourselves at how clever we are to get out of doing that old boring school work.

A couple of hours later, to our surprise, we realize the herder is nowhere in sight, leaving Rudigard and me alone with the cows.

Our hunger begins to dominate our thoughts. Playing hooky no longer seems like such a great idea after all.

"Do you know the way back?" Rudigard asked.

"No. Are you scared?"

Rudigard didn't answer.

Hunger eventually drives us to think we'll take a chance on finding our way back on our own. Just as soon as we get our courage up, fear sets in once more, and we decide we'd better wait for the herder.

We begin to look for berries or anything to eat. No luck; however, we had plenty of water to drink out of the stream that ran through the meadow. Hours pass. The sun begins to sink behind the mountain.

Finally, the herder comes for the cows. We are so relieved but do not approach the herder for fear we might be in trouble with him. We walk behind the cows down from the meadow.

Soon, we'd be home again. At some point, we realize the herder has brought the cows back to town on a different and unfamiliar route. We didn't know where we were or how we'd get home. If only we had gone to school, none of this would have happened. Now, we were lost *and* scared. We begin to think about the trouble we're in. It's long past the time we normally get home from school, and they'll probably all be out looking for us. It's not hard to figure out; we're in big trouble. With the help of several people we stop and ask on the street, we finally find our way back home. It's almost dark.

By the time I open my front door, I'm crying my eyes out, probably out of fear knowing full well I'm going to get a big whipping from my dad. He hears me and comes storming out of his sewing quarters down the hallway. He wasted no time showing his impatience and anger with me.

"Where have you been all day, young man?" he asks. "We've been worried ever since we got word that you were not in school today. Your mother has been out looking for you for hours. So, *where were you?*"

Through the tears and sobbing of a five-year-old, I tell him my long, hard luck story about how lost, hungry and afraid we were. I was hoping he might take pity on me, but no such luck. Without saying a word, he turns abruptly and heads back toward his sewing room. I know what's coming next; the dreaded leather strap. He quickly returned. There was no talking. After he gave me a whipping I will never forget, he then returned to his quarters, leaving me sitting alone sobbing. Unfortunately, he and I never had any kind of personal relationship or did father-son type activities together.

Compassion was definitely not on his radar. Fathers in those days (and particularly in my German culture) proudly accepted their role as *provider* while the role of mothers was that of taking responsibility for everything else; have the kids, raise the kids, teach the kids, manage the house, cook, clean, sew, wash clothes, take the kids to church and whatever else needed to be done. Roles were rigidly defined, and there were few or no exceptions, ever. Although my dad was a very hard working man, on occasion he met some of his men friends at the local brewery for a night out of letting a little steam off. He was quite a good singer and performed with the all-men's civic choir.

I'm still crying when my mom comes home. She is relieved I made it home safe and is definitely more sympathetic to my hard luck story I just told to my dad. She gives me a long reassuring hug, takes me into the kitchen and warms up leftovers she made earlier for supper. The apple strudel along with a big glass of milk for desert sure gave me a special sense of belonging again. She sits with me at the table until I talk and cry it all out. By now, I am exhausted, my tummy is full and I just want to go to bed. Thank goodness for the compassion and understanding of a loving mom.

Although tired and sleepy, I lay in bed for a while thinking about how good that apple strudel tasted and the enjoyment I always got out of helping my mom make the pastry, which was a two-person job. The process was always the same. The dough was placed on a round cutting board type table, "patted" out somewhat, then on opposite sides of the table we pulled equally in a circle to make sure the thickness was the same all around. It was always the same routine.

"Here, hold this bowl of filling for me while I brush the dough with butter," she'd say.

I always held the bowl where she couldn't see how much of the yummy mixture I ate. Well, I thought so anyway. She then took the bowl and poured the filling on to the dough. It was fun watching her roll the dough into a long snake-like pastry. She'd then slide it onto a large pan and place it in the oven. The only thing better than the smell of fresh pastry baking in the oven is eating it fresh out of the oven while it's still runny and gooey. I finally fell asleep dreaming about that apple strudel.

School Days
1936

I somehow made it through my kindergarten year. After a fun summer break filled with swimming, hiking and spending time with my cousins, it was on to the first grade. I learned my lesson in kindergarten, and now it was time to follow the rules and learn something.

Throughout the next few years, school was enjoyable. The Catholic priest came to our school and taught a one-hour religious class once a week. Sometimes, when the weather was good, he played soccer with us in his kilt rather than teaching religion.

Mr. Arnold, a close friend of my father, was my fourth grade teacher. One day we were out on break playing soccer. The bell rang, but I explained to my buddies that Mr. Arnold was a very close friend of my dad, and I was sure he wouldn't do anything to us if we just kept playing. Was I ever wrong! That man called us all in and gave all forty of us ten licks each with a paddle. I believe I lost some friends that day, and some even wanted to beat me up.

I think his favorite subject was history, and I didn't care one thing about history. At the end of the school year, to make sure I learned a good lesson, he flunked me for the year because I made such a poor grade in history. I always wondered if my dad had some influence on Dr. Arnold's decision. Believe me, the next school year I became very interested in school work, especially in history, and at the end of the school year I was promoted to the next grade level with an "A" average.

Personal and Political Changes

The Communist party continued to harass and make life difficult for the general population and for Germans in particular, constantly levying higher taxes in an attempt to control the population.

In April 1941, my father became very ill with pneumonia and passed away suddenly. I was eleven years old and now considered man of the house.

About two weeks after my father passed away, German troops entered Yugoslavia, put the Communist Party in its place and returned relative calm and peace to the country. Freedom of movement, along with the restructuring of a strangling city government and devastating tax levies and laws, made life more enjoyable for everyone.

Noticeable positive changes also came for us kids. I signed up for glider school in 1942 when I was twelve years old and joined the band and the Red Cross safety swimming school when I was fourteen.

In 1943, thousands more German troops ended up in Werschetz after their withdrawal from Greece. We exchanged stories and made a few dinars on the black market. They mostly exchanged Turkish cigarettes for grapes and other available food or goods. Things were really hopping for about two weeks; then they were reassigned to various fronts across Europe.

The original German troops remained there until 1944, when they too were reassigned to other warring zones on the eastern front, leaving Yugoslavia vulnerable to Russian invasion.

After they left, we found a lot of outdated military equipment, including rifles and ammo. Many of them had broken wood stocks, and they had pounded the barrels into the ground. No one wanted them, but I had my own ideas. I decided to take one of the rifles home. It just might come in handy one day. After cleaning the barrel and repairing the wood stock, I invited one of my friends over, as I didn't have the courage to pull the trigger by myself at thirteen years old. In our large open courtyard, I set up a target against a brick wall, and target practice began. We were quite pleased the rifle actually worked.

When one of the lady neighbors heard the shooting, she became upset and proceeded to express her displeasure with us. But as boys will be boys, we had just found this new toy and kept shooting. Next thing we knew she had reported us to the German soldiers at the base across the street. They told her we were not harming anyone and to leave us alone. When my mother heard what happened from the neighbor, she told me to get rid of the rifle. I finally convinced her that, since I was now the man of the house, we may need the rifle for protection. She made me promise not to shoot it in the courtyard anymore.

With my sister now living in Germany, mom and I had the house to ourselves. The financial burden of keeping the house up and paying taxes became very stressful to my mother. In late '43 and most of '44, we rented a bedroom to a sergeant by the name of Herr Kraus. He was also of German descent from Romania. His family owned a hat factory there and bought a lot of felt cones locally. He hired me to pick up his merchandise in my little wagon. Pickups were always after dark. I didn't ask questions, as I made more money in one pickup than my mother made all week working at the base across the street. Times were hard and, after all, I was the man of the house. In Herr Kraus's travels, he brought back sacks full of Italian shoes and clothes. It didn't take long to figure out he had a very lucrative international black market business going; however, I once overheard him tell someone that he was an attaché to an officer's unit.

Around the end of August, Herr Kraus moved out and informed us that Romania was now an ally of Russia. Hopefully he made it through the war. He was a very nice and generous person from a well-to-do family. To this day, I remain both thankful and grateful for his generosity and kindness. It made life much easier and more tolerable for my mother and me during difficult times.

Horror stories linger about mistreatment and missing Jews all across Europe. We hear such justification by the Nazis that the Jews are using special radios to provide information on troop strength, location and movement.

The one remaining radio station in Belgrade is now shut down. All newspapers are closed. Underground news reports that Hitler and the Nazis have been defeated on most fronts across Europe. And closer to home, retreating German soldiers report that the Russian Army is drawing closer and closer to invading our city. Deep fear sets in for both the known and unknown as war is now at our own doorstep.

Sister Hildegard, Rudy, mother Maria

My father, Julius Seemayer

Mother Maria, Uncle Julius, Aunt Tillie

Rudy and Sister Hildegard

My confirmation with Uncle Ignatz and friend

Aunt Tillie and Uncle Martin Huber

Cousins Hilde and Anne

CHAPTER 2

Escape on "The Last Train Out"

■■■

Fall 1944

URGENT MESSAGE FROM THE UNDERGROUND: Warning! *Russian front moving closer to Werschetz ….. **Invasion eminent!***

Without hesitation, on September 27, 1944, the order we hoped would never come was given: **Evacuate!**

In earlier planning for such an event, a group of parents, church leaders and city elders developed a plan to evacuate as many children as possible to safety by train. Space would be limited to children and a few teachers only. No parents allowed. Each child was required to bring a footlocker filled with flour, sugar, smoked meats and any other available nonperishable foodstuffs.

At first, my mother would not hear of letting me go. I had just turned fourteen years old, and there were only the two of us left to look after one another. However, after Uncle Julius and one of the teachers convinced her of the real dangers of getting captured by the Russians, she finally agreed to let me go. After all, the plan was for the children to be moved to safety then return after the war was over.

On September 31, everyone was instructed to bring their children to the station at 10:00 the next morning to catch *The Last Train Out*.

Uncle Julius picked my mother and me up around 8:00 a.m. We loaded my luggage and footlocker on to the horse-drawn wagon and arrived at the train station about thirty minutes later.

Over one thousand children, including both boys and girls ranging in age from nine to fourteen years old, along with school teachers and Catholic nurses who volunteered for the mission, were finally loaded onto the train. The plan was to resume our education as soon as we arrived safely in Germany a few days later. It was made very clear that parents would not be allowed to leave on this train; however, to everyone's surprise, just before the train pulled out of the station, it was announced that any parent still on the train at that time would be permitted to leave with the children.

I begged my mother to go, but she explained,

"All I have with me is my purse and the clothes on my back."

She took me by the shoulders, looked directly into my eyes and in a somewhat stern, yet comforting voice, continued.

"Don't worry, Rudi. You have been the man of the house for two years—you are strong, and I know you will be okay."

"But what about you? What will happen to you?" I questioned.

"Don't worry about me. Just take care of yourself and, before you know it, we'll be together again."

She then hugged and held me tight for an unusually long time, said goodbye, turned and walked toward the exit.

A very short time later, the conductor gives three long whistles, and the train begins to move ever so slowly away from the station. I quickly race to the platform side of the train and hang outside the window in hopes of seeing her in the crowd. Finally, I spot her following the train. I hear her calling my name,

"Rudi, Rudi, Rudi."

The train quickly picks up considerable speed. As it pulls farther and farther away, the station and people become smaller and smaller until, soon, they are completely out of sight.

I fear for her safety and wonder if I'll ever see her again.

CHAPTER 3

From Werschetz to Germany

■ ■ ■

OCTOBER 1944

THE CALCULATED RISK OF TRAVELING through Tito's partisan territories was of great concern; however, with the eminent invasion of the Russians, there was no other choice.

Not long after our journey began, one of the officials discovered my rifle. In a gruff voice, he asked:

"Young man, is that your rifle?"

"Yes, this is my rifle."

"You are not allowed to have this weapon. Hand it over," the official barked.

One of the teachers sitting nearby hears the conversation and steps in.

"We might need this rifle to defend ourselves, so I think we should keep it."

The official reluctantly agrees. I keep my rifle.

Dangers Ahead

Thank goodness, none of us had any idea of the dangers that lay ahead. From what we were told, we were going on a long train ride to Germany where we'd be safe. There, we'd continue our education until things settled down in Werschetz. Then we'd pack up and go back home.

At approximately noon, we arrive in Belgrade. The train ride was fun with all those kids on board. What a great start to an exciting adventure. Then suddenly all hell breaks loose. With the deafening sound of the continuous train whistle, one blast after another, along with the screeching of the brakes, everyone begins to scream. It felt as though we just entered the twilight zone. After what seemed like an eternity, the train finally comes to an abrupt stop with a strong jerking motion. We all run to the windows to see what's happening. The train is sitting on a high embankment just at the edge of the Danube River.

Teachers do their best to calm everyone down and reassure us that everything is okay, but, after what just happened, I don't think any of us are convinced.

We waited anxiously. Finally, teachers made their way through each car announcing that the main section of the Danube River Bridge had been bombed and destroyed by the Americans (flying out of bases from either Italy or North Africa) and that the Danube was mined in an effort to slow down traffic, including the evacuation of German troops. We didn't have any idea exactly what any of that meant, but we understood enough to realized that our nice little train ride *get-away* had definitely taken an unexpected, uncertain and troublesome turn. After sitting there for a while, we were ordered to unload the train and board one of the large open ferries crossing the river. Kidlike, we begin throwing suitcases out of the windows rather than carrying them downhill. Most of them pop open upon impact, scattering clothing and personal items over the length of the train. After gathering and repacking what belongings we could fit into our suitcases, we carry them about four hundred yards down to the ferry.

Unfortunately, there was no room for our trunks of food. We were told to leave them on the train. Once loaded on the ferry along with other civilians and German troops, we were off to the other side, which was approximately a fourth of a mile wide at that point. We were all scared. And rightfully so. The current was swift causing the ferry to be tossed about, and we were terrified that one of the mines floating down river might hit and blow us up. But we had no choice. We had to get across to the other side. The Russians were coming our way toward Belgrade.

A strong steel cable stretched from one side of the Danube to the other. Ferries, which looked more like barges, were attached to the cable and pulled across to the other side by strong and capable hands on deck. It was a terrifying experience. But thank goodness, we all made it across safely to the other side.

The sound of the train engine back across the Danube gets our attention, and we turn around to see what's happening. We all watch as the train is backed up a few hundred yards, stops, and then put into forward motion. As the train moves closer and closer to the bombed-out bridge, we watch in horror and disbelief. It appears the train is being dumped into the Danube—with all our food and extra equipment on board. *It happened just that way.* Although we were told this was done to deny the Russians use of all that food and use of the train, it didn't make us feel any better.

There we stood, a thousand children on the bank of the Danube River, out in the open, with no food or transportation. Although teachers continued to assure us all would be okay, we were in no way convinced. Many of the younger children were crying for their parents. It was time for us older ones to put on our *brave face* and do whatever we could to comfort these scared young children.

After waiting for some time, we hear the engine of a train in the distance coming from another direction. We're told it's the train coming to take us on our journey. We were excited and relieved. Shortly after the train loads and we're on our way, we hear a tremendous explosion in the direction of the Danube. Later, we learned that one of the ferries we crossed on earlier was blown up by a mine floating down the river.

The mood changed rather quickly. Things got considerably quieter. Our little fun adventure had turned into something quite different from what we expected, and we had only been gone from home a few hours. It was all too confusing.

Before long, one of the teachers announced that we would soon be crossing into Hungary. He further advised:

"There is a possibility we may come under air attack. For this reason, the train will be traveling at a low rate of speed so it can stop quickly allowing everyone to jump off the train as quickly as possible and seek cover in nearby bushes or trees. We expect the older ones to help the younger ones to safety."

We all sit in silence, almost scared to death, not knowing what to expect. (Our train could easily be mistaken for German troops on the move.)

The new train arrives. And a welcome sight it is. We quickly learn that there is food aboard and the train will stop during mealtimes for us to eat.

We make it through Hungary safely; next stop is Vienna, Austria. For two days we feel like kids again enjoying ourselves at the zoo and taking in all the sites around the city. Even as children, we enjoy the magnificent architecture and historical sites Vienna had to offer. Little did we know, from that day forward, our lives would be drastically changed forever.

Vienna was used as a staging area to divide all the kids into age groups for the sake of schooling. From there, each group would be sent to different parts of Austria and Germany. We had no prior knowledge of this plan. Once again, we find ourselves saying an unexpected sad goodbye to our friends and cousins.

My group of one hundred and five boys was sent to Michelau, near Lichtenfels in Germany. Once we arrive at the school camp, I finally have to give up my rifle. I'm told it is needed on the front.

Our housing was a large hall with a balcony on the outside, which was converted into a temporary mess hall. Bunk beds were two and three levels high, and community wash rooms were set up at one end of the building.

Life in this small town was very dull. Kid-like activities were run by a twenty-year-old ex-SS Army officer who had lost one of his arms on the Russian front. He wore a small pistol on his belt to look impressive.

The first order given was to shave everyone's head to control lice. When we heard this, five of us decided we'd leave the camp and go out on our own. However, we didn't make it very far as an Army Nazi came after us, shooting in the air and scaring us half to death.

Daily American air raids constantly had us retreating into the woods for cover. After a while, we learn by the sound of the plane engines if they were empty or loaded with bombs. The intensity of the air raids increased to the point that our school officials decide to transfer our group out of the path of the constant bombardment to a safer location. One hundred miles to the west was Frankfurt, sixty miles to the east was Bamberg, and one hundred eighty miles south was Munich. None of those were good choices. We loaded onto a train and headed to a beautiful remote area in Czechoslovakia.

Our accommodations were at a four-story confiscated resort hotel not far from Pilsen and Prague. Schooling quickly resumed, and life seemed pleasant and almost normal again.

While exploring the building one day, we discover a door going into the attic. A sign hung on the door that said in bold letters, **KEIN EINGANG** (no entry). And from the looks of the heavy duty lock, we figure there must be something of value behind that door. Our curiosity quickly outweighs our fear of getting caught and, before long, we gain entry. To our delight, over a hundred pairs of snow skis were stored there. Our risk was well worth taking. Luckily, we didn't get in trouble. From then on, we were allowed to ski almost every day after our school work was finished. It felt great to have fun again.

Also found in the attic were large containers of flour, sugar and other baking supplies. We finally figure out how to rig up a small cooker and begin to make pancakes in our room. I'm not sure if it was a lack of cooking skills or something else that went terribly wrong with the make-shift "stovetop" cooker on our very first attempt. Unfortunately for us, the smell and smoke from the burning pancakes tipped off the officials. We were in big trouble as strict house rules prohibited anyone from cooking in their room—and for good reason. It was easy to see the hotel could easily be burned to the ground with such an electrical malfunction from a small appliance rigged up by a bunch of teenage boys.

Since I was the instigator of this undertaking, I got a good beating by the hotel manager right in front of one of my teachers. It's understandable, from that day forward, I didn't care much for that old coot. The pancake operations ceased after that, but we continued to boil eggs stolen from the hotel manager's hen house.

On weekends, small groups of us were allowed to board a train and visit Prague. This was a beautiful western-type city steeped in rich endless history. The architecture of its magnificent churches and buildings reminded me of Vienna.

We spent hours strolling about the downtown area visiting various stores and shops. It was surprising to see that one could buy sardines and various other canned foods without rations. However, little good it did us; we had no money.

This was unheard of in Germany. Rationing began in 1942 all over Europe. Life became very tough and chaotic by the end of the war. No one government was in charge, food and goods were practically nonexistent and any money still in existence was of no value.

Our schooling and skiing activities continued until about mid-March when we were visited by a company of German troops. They took up one whole floor of the hotel to rest a few days before going back to the Russian front, which was only about one hundred miles away. Watching troop activities was a welcomed diversion for us. One thing we found particularly amusing was the way they "drove" their jeeps. Because of extreme shortages of gasoline at this point, they pushed the vehicles for a good running start before turning on the engine. They also turned the engine off and coasted down hills.

As the Russians came closer and closer to our camp, we were told to pack our belongings and get ready to board army trucks coming for us. Once again, we are on the move running from the Russians in search of safety. But this time, things were different; we would migrate closer to the advancing American troops.

In fear of air attacks, we left around midnight and traveled throughout the night. At one point, the drivers took the wrong turn as signs were switched by the Czech underground. They also tossed u-nails onto the roads to create flat tires and slow down movement. Heading the wrong direction would have landed us in the hands of the Commies. Thank goodness, our drivers sensed something was wrong and relied on their compasses to keep us on the right track. Around daybreak, we arrive at our new home, which is an old gym or hall in Sudetenland, an area belonging to Czechoslovakia that fell to Germany after the takeover in 1939.

We are informed that American troops are within days of our present location, and the end of the war was eminent! Everyone is jubilant, although we are not sure what that will mean to us directly.

Our building was built on the slope of a hill overlooking the railroad station and two abandoned bunkers from WWI. The first bunker was located about two hundred yards in front of our building.

The Americans arrive. They first target and destroy the rail station and then go after the bunker closest to our building. Their first round misses its target and hits between the bunker and our building. We're now under full attack by the Americans. We might not be so lucky the next round.

"Run for your life!" someone yells out, as if we need prompting.

As we run out of the building for the woods, we're each handed three small potatoes. Once in the woods, and after the shelling settles down for a while, we are informed that our food supply is virtually gone and that we should conserve what food we have left.

Several of the boys were sick with colds, and one little fellow was critically ill and running a high temperature. When we left the building under heavy artillery fire, we were only able to grab a few of our belongings. It was freezing cold, and we didn't know how long we would be hiding out. We only knew these sick boys had to have blankets to keep them warm. Still under intermittent heavy fire, one of my friends and I volunteer to go back for blankets. We ran as fast as we could all the way there and back. On the way back, I am hit by shrapnel that went through my lower pant leg but, luckily, didn't touch my skin. That was a close call.

That same day, mid-morning, the American infantry takes the nearby town and, for us, *thanks be to God*, the war is over. We are more than relieved and happy to fall into the hands of the Americans rather than the Russians.

We move back into our building, and we're starving by now. With caution, we venture into the town where all the American troops are milling around. They are surprised and intrigued to see all us little hungry, straggly German-speaking refugees coming out of the woods. It didn't take long to make friends, although we all spoke a different language. They fed us until our bellies almost popped open. How good that food tasted. How great it felt to feel full again.

We quickly start a business with the soldiers. They wanted fresh eggs, and we wanted chocolate candy bars. One fresh egg bought two to three candy bars, and we gave the farmers one candy bar for three eggs. What a life! Good times were here again! We hadn't even seen a candy bar in at least two years. Much of our food in the next few days was traded with the Americans. On about the fourth day of all this wheeling and dealing, several of my friends and I were walking around and just happened up on some GIs cooking something in a big iron pot. It sure smelled good. In fact, it smelled just like— chocolate! We hid in some bushes nearby and watched. They stirred and stirred whatever was in that pot, set it aside off the fire and walked back inside the tent. We waited for some time to see if they were going to return. Finally, we decided it was time to make our move. We each carried a big spoon in our back pocket just in case we ever found something to eat. As we come closer and look down into the pot, we discover, for sure and certain, it is chocolate pudding! We grab our spoons out of our pockets and begin eating the pudding. In a short time, we drop our spoons and began to scoop it up with our hands. That chocolate pudding was the best thing we had ever eaten.

We ate and ate until we couldn't eat any more. The GIs never came out of the tent. In retrospect, they either left it out for us to enjoy, knowing how hungry we were, or perhaps, once they saw us digging in, they just left us in peace to fill our hungry bellies. Whatever the case, there are just no words to describe how good that chocolate pudding tasted to all of us. We were a bunch of mighty hungry little refugees getting our fill of something so good.

THE WAR HAS ENDED, BUT WHAT NOW?
CZECHOSLOVAKIA – MAY 1945

We are refugees; most of us around fourteen years in age, displaced persons without a country, no parents, uncertain future and no one to take responsibility for us. Although we are all of German descent, there is no longer a German government, so we were pretty much on our own. For the next few days, we feel totally lost; that is, until the American GIs begin to help us through this transition period. I remember my first big dream and goal after the war ended.

"Someday, I want to be an American soldier."

Over the next few days, we watched and listened to try and keep up with what was going on. Everything changed minute by minute sometimes. German officers and soldiers were now prisoners of war and were questioned daily. Many German officers lost their nice leather boots to American soldiers then were told to freely walk away, barefoot. The Americans let all German prisoners go free, but the question was where would they go? What would they find? Were their loved ones still alive? Did their homes and any part of life they once knew exist any longer? It was sad times for everyone with so much loss and uncertainty.

The total confusion and chaos of the next three weeks was a difficult time for everyone. On May 5, 1945, the section of Sudetenland we were in was officially signed over to Czechoslovakia under Russian rule. **And we were caught on the wrong side of the border.** Anyone crossing the border back into Bavaria had to have properly signed papers. We are Volksdeutschers; German from foreign lands, displaced persons with no country to return to and no one specific to turn to for help. It is absolutely impossible to imagine that, after all we've gone through to survive the war, we are now caught on the wrong side of the border and about to fall into the hands of Russian rule.

If anyone ever doubted the power of divine intervention, well, it's time to start believing! We will never know exactly how it happened, but we will be forever grateful and owe our lives to the American officials who, on that last day, at 9:00 a.m., one hour before the official exchange took place, were led to sign and deliver papers to us assuring our safe passage across the border into Germany. What happened that day was truly a miracle. At the last minute, we were delivered out of bondage or death as German prisoners, even though we were children, in the hands of Russians and communist rule in Czechoslovakia.

With two horses and wagons, we quickly load up what few belongings we possess and head for the German/Czech border which is only three miles away. As the two old half starved horses struggle to carry the load, we all pitch in and help push the carts (and horses) up the hill across the *finish line*; over the border into Germany. Thank God, we made it.

Although it was a joyous moment for us personally, it was also a very difficult situation to go through. There were hundreds of starving people on foot, some with small children, some on canes and some with broken limbs being almost dragged along, all after the same thing; getting across the border into freedom—or whatever was on the other side.

In all the chaos and confusion, most didn't have any idea where they going or what they were going to do once they got there.

During our journey on foot toward Bavaria, we camped out nights in farmers' barns and rummaged for food along the way. We survived many days on one potato. Occasionally, we found wild spinach, which usually grew around outhouses. Half of the kids kept dysentery. We all looked half-starved.

During the last few months of the war, we had very little schooling. Nonetheless, the teachers who were still with us were of great help if nothing more than to keep us together somehow. It's a miracle everyone survived.

Four days later, weary and even hungrier, we arrived at our destination; a small village near Passau in Bavaria and were given army barracks to live in. We finally had a "home" with real beds and facilities to bathe in. We even had facilities to wash our clothes. Our old ragged clothes should have been thrown away, but we washed and kept them since that was all we had.

For the first few days, town folks provided us with three simple meals each day. About three weeks later, one of my friends and I decided to roam the countryside looking for a job with a farmer who would pay us in food. One farmer finally hired us in exchange for food only—after all, who needed Reichsmarks? There was nothing to buy anywhere. I lasted about a week in the fields working like a mule, turning hay in the daytime and cleaning out barns in the evening. During lunch one day, I tell my friend I am going back to camp with the boys before that old farmer works me to death. I leave. Upon my return, the boys are all taking a nap at three o'clock in the afternoon. Man, that's the life for me. What was I thinking???

The following day, hunger begins to get the best of me again, and I come up with another idea. We knew there had to be fish in the streams all around us, but we had no fishing gear. A lot of low-lying fields in Germany had shallow trenches or small creeks that drained into the rivers. If there are fish in rivers, then surely there must be a few fish in these shallow trenches. Right? Right! As we proceed to walk through the trenches, fish begin to jump all over the place.

All we have to do is slap them out of the air onto the bank and gather them up. From that day forward, we never went hungry again.

Our schooling continued to some extent until June. As soon as our summer vacation started, we began to travel in various directions looking over the countryside and Passau which was a beautiful old city with a population of approximately 100,000 inhabitants. On one trip there, I went to get my official identification papers. Trains were so overloaded that many young people sat on top of the rail cars inhaling smoke from locomotives. When I arrive in Passau at 10:00 a.m., I walk to the courthouse to get my legal papers taken care of. There were lines everywhere. It took up to two to three hours to get waited on.

By the time I finished there, I returned to the station only to find I had missed my train. This meant I would have to spend the night in the train station. Meanwhile, I met a nice old lady who learned of my situation. She invited me to her home, cooked a nice meal and gave me a comfortable bed to sleep in. Could this be luck, or is she another angel on high looking after me? I'm so grateful and appreciative of everyone who helped me along this oftentimes lonesome, long and hard journey of survival. My friend and I wrote postcards for many years. She was like a mother or grandmother to me.

That summer in June of 1945, I was almost fifteen years old. I didn't know if any of my family made it through the war, but it was time to make an all-out effort to find out.

CHAPTER 4

The Search for Family

■ ■ ■

1945

GERMANY WAS OCCUPIED BY THE US, Britain, France and Russia. In Berlin, each of these same four powers occupied specific sectors of the city. Russia wasted no time in closing down all roads, ground traffic and supplies leading into Berlin through the Russian zone. Both Churchill's and Patton's previous warnings that Stalin was not to be trusted were validated by this very serious action. The Russians were warned to open the border but would not comply. All those in the Russian zone were now cut off from the outside world with very little food or necessities for survival. They needed help, desperately.

The US quickly put a plan in place to use bombers still stored in Britain to deliver food and supplies inside the Russian zone by using an airstrip at a US base. Once the Russians realized they could not stop the US from getting through, road restrictions were eventually lifted. It didn't take long before reports got out about the overall mistreatment, brutality, rape and thievery the Russians imposed upon those in their zone.

The ordinary citizens of Germany living normal lives, as in any other country, suffered in many ways because of the politics, madness and brutality of Hitler and his Nazi regime. Personal and business property, as well as infrastructure, was decimated. There was widespread hunger and suffering and, to make matters worse, the Mark was devalued from ten to one. In general, food, hard drugs, Nazi gold, and other necessities and supplies were sold on the black market, which was controlled by the "Stase" (new corrupt German police) and the East Germany Russian Communist police with headquarters in Partenkirchen in the Bavarian Alps.

For several months after the war ended, I remained in school camp in Bavaria near Passau. From time to time, we all discussed how or when we might try and contact relatives. I remember having a conversation with some of my teachers about going to live with my sister. Naturally, they wanted verification of my sister's exact location and proof that she could take care of me properly. Unfortunately, mail service and other means of communication were still very limited. But I wanted to try. Through everything that happened since I left Werschetz in 1943, I managed to save my sister's address. I wrote my letter:

> *Dear Hilde, I am in a refugee school camp in Bavaria. I hope you are okay. The school will allow me to leave if I can find a relative to live with. Yours is the only address I have. Can I come live with you? I hope you get this letter. Your brother, Rudi*

For weeks, I waited. Several months went by. No answer. I didn't know if she made it through the war—or maybe she just didn't get my letter. Food and supplies were in short supply. Maybe she was simply not able to feed and take care of me. There was no way of knowing.

Then one day, one of my teachers called me to his office. I thought I was in trouble again, but, as soon as I entered the room, I could see he was very excited about something.

"Rudi, here is a letter from your sister," and handed it to me to read.

Dear Rudi, I am so happy to hear you made it through the war. Please inform your school that I would like for you to come live with me. Let me know when I might expect you. Love, Your Sister Hilde

My teacher told me he would discuss the matter with the other teachers and let me know. About a week later, I was called in for a meeting. Although they were somewhat apprehensive about allowing me to go on such a long train ride by myself, I was given permission to leave the school and go live with my sister in Hasedorf in northern Germany.

January 1946

It was freezing cold. Warm shoes and clothing were scarce. The school packed me a little sack lunch with half a sandwich and some kind of dried fruit. One of the teachers accompanied me to the station, bought me a one-way ticket and got me settled on the train. I was the only one in that car for the longest time. There was no heat on the train at all, and the clothes I had on were not of much help to keep me warm. It was a very long and miserable trip. However, I had much to look forward to once I arrived. I wonder if she'd heard anything about our mother or other relatives.

After ten hours on the train, half frozen, hungry and thirsty, I finally reached Hasedorf. Hilde and some of her friends were at the station to meet me. What an incredible reunion that was. After all, we had both survived the war and were somehow together again. The last time I saw her was in the summer of 1943 when she came home to Werschetz for a month when I was thirteen years old.

The area my sister lived in was occupied by the British under similar conditions as the American zone. However, the shortage of food and supplies existed everywhere. Most girls, including Hilde, dated British soldiers. The soldiers were good to provide them with food they smuggled from their own military kitchens. Money was also in short supply.

Hilde lived in a poorly insulated one-room barrack. We used an old wood burner for both cooking and heating when firewood or burning materials were available. When wood was in short supply, I took responsibility to find coal or turf that had been cut and dried for such use.

After thawing out, resting a few days and eating some nourishing food, it was back to school for me again. Hilde continued to work as a professional seamstress.

By September of that year, farmers were hard at work harvesting their potato crops. Since money was worthless, everything was traded or bartered on the black market all over

Germany. Three hundred pounds of potatoes could be traded for a pair of shoes.

Although signs went up all over the countryside warning of a three-year jail sentence for anyone getting caught stealing potatoes, times were hard and I knew what I had to do. I made several trips to the field daily on my bicycle. Even though the threat of a three-year jail sentence was frightening, the possibility of starving outweighed that fear.

If only I didn't have to ride by the Bergermeister's (mayor's) house with my full sacks of stolen potatoes. Getting caught by the Bergermeister was an added fear. So I came up with a plan. I'd carefully stuff hay in my sack to make it look like rabbit food. After all, many people raised rabbits for food, so maybe, just maybe, my scheme would work and no one would suspect I was carrying bags of stolen potatoes.

That season, I "helped myself" to 900 pounds of potatoes—just enough for a pair of shoes and a decent food supply for Hilde and me for a couple of months through the winter.

Everything went great until one of my trips to the field. I spotted a farmer about a hundred yards away. It was plain to see he was holding a shotgun pointed directly at me— just *waiting*! As soon as I spot him, a different kind of survival instinct takes over. I drop my bag of potatoes and take off running like a jack rabbit through the plowed field, carrying my bicycle over my head the whole time, thinking how much worse it might be stuck in a jail cell for three years!

The farmer begins to chase me but never even gets close. When I reach the road, I drop my bicycle to the ground as I'm running and mount it just like trick riders mount their horses in Wild West shows. I take off like lightning. Looking back, I'm sure I could have easily won the Olympics bicycling race on that day. That was my last trip to the potato fields. After my potato harvesting was all done, I became very ill with a high fever that lasted for a week.

My sister's girlfriend next door dated a British GI whose name was Jimmy. Jimmy and I became friends. He passed cigarettes to me through cracks in the walls. We all learned to accept a steady diet of dehydrated foods, including powdered eggs. The milk we drank, when we could get it, was known as "Blue Henry," as all the cream had been totally removed, transforming the taste, color and food value to little more than water. There was an old saying in those days that even pigs would have left home if they were fed the same food sold to the people.

During those times, we could not have survived if it weren't for the black market and help from the allied British and American GIs. We would have been totally lost. The poor souls living in the Russian zone were not so lucky.

We still had not heard a word from our mother. All efforts to contact her or learn anything of her whereabouts had failed. Communication, including mail, especially from other countries, was still very inadequate.

After hearing how badly the Russians treated the locals in Berlin, we couldn't bear to think what might have happened to our mother and other relatives who didn't get out after the Russians invaded Yugoslavia within hours after our escape on The Last Train Out.

In search of our mother and other relatives, Hilde learned that Aunt Tillie (my mother's sister) and her husband, Uncle Martin, and their two children were living near Stuttgart in southern Germany.

Tragedy Strikes Again
January 1947

Hilde and some of her friends took a bus trip. On their way back home, there was a terrible accident. The bus collided with a fast moving train. Hilde was killed instantly.

I was now sixteen years old. Everything was still in short supply, including money, and I had no idea how or where to begin making funeral arrangements. This was a very confusing and traumatic time for me. My life's journey seemed to have come to a dead end. I felt totally helpless and defeated.

At the suggestion of one of Hilde's close friends, I was finally able to contact my aunt and uncle in Stuttgart. They were happy to hear from me but saddened by the news of Hilde's death. Without hesitation, they assured me they'd come to be by my side and help with the burial arrangements. The next day, Aunt Tillie and my eighteen-year-old cousin, Frank, arrived by train. This was a very sad day for all of us, although we were all comforted being together again.

We visited and had something to eat. After the long train ride, they were tired so we went to bed fairly early. Morning came, and Frank and I began making arrangements for Hilde's funeral service. We were raised Catholic, so our first stop was to talk to the local Priest about the burial service. Somewhere in the conversation, he found out Hilde had a child out of wedlock during the war, and because of Catholic belief, the priest refused to perform the service. Sadly, the baby died soon after her birth. We contacted a number of priests who refused to bury her despite our desperate pleas for help. Not only was I suffering the personal loss of my sister, I felt totally helpless, lost and betrayed by the church.

One of our British soldier friends heard about the difficulties we were experiencing with burial services. Soon after that, someone from British headquarters came to inform me that a Catholic Priest from Poland who was serving in their division would perform the service. This seemed like a small miracle after all the difficulties and heartache we suffered trying to get my sister laid to rest with a proper burial.

After the service was over, I thanked all of our friends who had helped Hilde and me through all the hard times, said goodbye and began our walk back to the barracks. In my silence, I couldn't keep from thinking about my dad dying when I was only eleven, now my sister is gone, and all efforts to find out what happened to our mother had failed.

Aunt Tillie broke the silence with a big surprise to me. "Rudy, your Uncle Martin and I talked it over and it has been decided. You will come live with us. There is a three o'clock train leaving for Stuttgart, and we can make it if we hurry."

I had not even had time to think about my own future—where I would go, what I would do or how I would make it on my own.

This was another defining moment in my life. Once again, somehow, angels were there to rescue me; to take me in and love and care for me as if I were their own. Although I hadn't had time to think about it, the idea of going to live with them was a huge relief.

As soon as we arrive back at the barracks, I quickly pack my personal belongings that fit in to one small cloth bag which closed with a drawstring, and the three of us quickly head for the train station.

We no sooner get settled in to our seats when the train gives three loud whistles and, with a jolt, we begin to move slowly away from Hasedorf station. I sat silently for quite some time just staring out the window. The deafening sound of the clickety-clack of the wheels passing over the trestles soon gave way to thoughts that took me back home to the day I said my final goodbye to my mother. And now, I'm leaving Hilde behind.

I'm not sure how long I sat there by myself, but I was glad when Frank came and sat beside me. He sat silently for a short time then began to talk about fun times we had as kids.

"Remember when I used to come visit you on school breaks and helped you fight those Serbian kids?"

One story led to another and, before long, Aunt Tillie joined in and we were all laughing remembering the good times. The long train ride to Stuttgart turned out to be an incredible transition period for all of us going from times of great sadness and loss to a journey of renewal—of family being together again.

Although it was very late when we arrived in Stuttgart, Uncle Martin and Anne were there to greet us. We were all so happy to see one another. Uncle Martin's big smile and bear hug instantly gave me a sense of reassurance and confidence that everything was going to be okay from then on.

Unbeknown to me at the time, Uncle Martin already had big plans for me.

CHAPTER 5

Seeking Greener Grass on the Other Side

■■■

JOURNEY THROUGH SCHOOL TO IMMIGRATION

IT IS COMFORTING TO HAVE the love and support of family as I try to make some sense of and come to terms with all that happened since I fled Yugoslavia. Sometimes, there are just no good answers.

But now, what could be greater? Living with my mother's sister, Aunt Tillie, my Uncle Martin whom I love and respect, and my two cousins, Frank and Anne with whom I spent summers harvesting grapes and having fun back home.

After taking a little time off to readjust my life a bit, I'm now back in school. Frank and Anne are both majoring in business administration while I decide to study horticulture.

In Yugoslavia, Uncle Martin was a very successful businessman distributing heavy farm machinery and equipment. Over the years, he established excellent credit and strong ties with a number of banks, which allowed his company to grow and prosper. At that time, he owned the second-largest farm machinery retail operation in all of Yugoslavia.

After the war, food supply was in very big demand in Germany. My uncle decided to start up another farm equipment company to meet the demand of growers.

He sold tractors and the likes one year in advance, before factory productions actually started up again. Demand was high. For this, he received bonuses from farmers such as completely processed pigs (smoked meats, hams, sausage and such). When the order was ready, Frank and I traveled by train to pick up the meat in heavy suitcases. This sort of "trade" or bartering was illegal and could lead to jail time for anyone getting caught participating in such activities. However, times were hard, and the short supply of foodstuffs on the open market motivated individuals to create clever ways to provide food for their families.

The old man briefed Frank and me thoroughly before our first pick up. He explained the importance of denying ownership of the luggage if authorities asked to open them.

Frequently, I was sent out with a bottle of schnapps to exchange for coffee from one of the US Army bases. That sort of home brew was made in garages everywhere and proved to be an excellent commodity on the black market in exchange for food and hard-to-get items.

1947 – Stuttgart, Germany

I was seventeen years old and in school where I made lots of friends. Since I left home at the age of fourteen, I became very independent and self reliant and thought I had all the answers to everything. What I didn't know was that my uncle had his own plans for me.

I worked very hard in school, but, because of all the school we lost during and after the war while in camps, much of our schooling suffered or had been lost altogether. After only three weeks in horticulture school, as hard as I tried, I just could not keep up with the studies. I quit. And now, I have to go back and tell Uncle of my decision.

When I finally got up the nerve to tell him, he calmly explained to me that if I wanted to have a chance for a good life, I would have to leave Germany. And that would require that I get a good education just to get on a list to apply for immigration to America, land of freedom and opportunity. Without blinking an eye or any kind of warning, he then proceeded to slap my face, with one hand then the other, back and forth. He definitely got my attention. Without question, I returned to school. I can't say it was ever easy for me, but I just kept thinking about how my Aunt and Uncle took me in, cared enough to send me to school, and were smart enough to lay out a path for success on my behalf. How could I disappoint them? How could I disappoint myself at this point?

College Graduation
1951

Finally, it was graduation time. However, graduation depended upon passing the final written and technical exam. On exam day, I show up early at 7:00 a.m. The test began at 7:30 and lasted until 6:00 p.m. that evening.

The next week of waiting was most stressful. I went from feeling confident I had done well and would graduate, allowing me to move forward with plans to immigrate to America, to feeling doubtful and fearful that I'd have to repeat certain courses, delaying my big plans.

Finally, after what seemed a lifetime of waiting, a large brown envelope comes in the mail. It's from the school, addressed to me. Everyone gathers around as Uncle Martin slowly opens my envelope. The solemn look on his face only lasts a few seconds. The waiting is over. His change of expression begins with a smile that gets bigger and bigger, and soon he bursts into almost a big belly laugh that sends us all rejoicing and celebrating. Then he reads the most important part of the letter aloud.

"Rudolf Seemayer has successfully fulfilled all requirements for graduation from Gartner (Horticulture) School."

My three long years of hard work and commitment, along with that *special* kind of encouragement from Uncle Martin and the love and support of my family, have finally paid off. I am now one giant step closer to securing my future.

All through my school years, the economy and life in general throughout Germany continued to improve. It was a good time to find employment. One of the professors at the horticulture school owned a huge nursery; however, he had quite a reputation for working his employees beyond reason. And yet, a letter of recommendation from him at the end of employment at his company was quite valuable. So I decided to interview with him. At the interview, he asks,

"Do you think you can exist under my harsh working conditions?"

Being of strong and sound mind and full of energy and enthusiasm, I accept his challenge. I was eager to get to work.

One of their primary sources of income was replanting cemetery plots three times a year with seasonal flowers, perennials, shrubs and other suitable plants. I could not imagine spending the rest of my life working primarily in cemeteries and, besides, what would it be like working there in the dark?

Other duties while there included working in the vegetable fields, planting and watering. Across from this field, approximately one hundred yards, was an American military base that caught my attention, especially the activities of these GIs playing baseball, jacking around and having a good time while I was sweating, breathing hard and working in the dirt shoveling *fertilizer.*

Talk about *the grass being greener on the other side of the fence.* Well, I made up my mind right then and there that someday, I was going to become part of this group with seemingly nothing to do but have a great time playing games and standing guard, looking great in their uniforms. Their lives seemed so carefree compared to what I had been doing. I didn't know how I'd get there, but that lifestyle definitely appealed to me, and I'd figure it out. All of these thoughts at that time seemed only but a dream. However, this was the second time I had this same dream; the first being just as the war ended when US troops fed us chocolate pudding and miraculously arranged for proper papers to be signed just in the nick of time to get us out of the communist sector of Czechoslovakia and across the border into safety and freedom in Germany.

My uncle's farming machinery business was in full operation as his bank loans were all approved the previous year. His new office building and warehouse were now complete. I didn't have much time off from my new job to visit family, but it sure was enjoyable to be there whenever possible. After about three weeks at my new job, my relatives and I got into a conversation about the terrible working conditions. At Uncle Martin's suggestion, they all agreed that I should quit this job and move away from the cemetery while I was still alive.

The following week, my uncle made an appointment near his place of business with one of the largest green house concerns in southern Germany. I joyfully and immediately quit my job not at all concerned with what my boss thought of me, knowing there was a good and promising life beyond his gates.

Things were looking up as my uncle's chauffer drove me to my interview appointment the following Monday. I met the president of the company, a delightful old gentleman in his late sixties. We had an enjoyable meeting, I got the job and with a half smile, he intimated that my physical condition should be excellent after working at my previous job.

Uncle Martin was so proud of me getting the job. He announced that night at dinner that he would talk with my friend Peter, his warehouse manager, about me moving in to the warehouse apartment with him. Peter agreed, and life suddenly was again very meaningful and enjoyable. Not only did I have a new job, I had a new rent-free apartment to share with my friend Peter. The next day, Uncle presented me with a new bicycle for my independent commute back and forth to work.

Peter did all the cooking, and I paid him for the food on a weekly basis. But there was one thing I could not figure out. After going to bed at 10:00 or 11:00 p.m., I'd hear him get up at 1:00 and again at 3:00 a.m. almost every night. My curiosity finally got the best of me and I asked him what was going on. He confessed that sooner or later he'd have to tell me and proceeded to show me his secret operation. He had a still in one of the locked back rooms making schnapps out of prunes. He was changing and corking the full schnapps bottles then cleaning up so that my uncle's staff wouldn't find out. Needless to say, I promised to keep my mouth shut and enjoyed a swig every now and then free of charge. I must admit the high alcoholic content of this schnapps could power an automobile or farm equipment engine. Life was really good.

June 1951

Unbeknown to me, Uncle Martin went to Frankfurt to meet an American gentleman he heard of, originally from Hungary also of German descent, by the name of Wagner. Mr. Wagner lived in Brooklyn, New York, and sponsored many post-war European displaced persons to the United States.

Immigration laws were very strict at that time. The first step toward immigrating to the US was simply getting an appointment to make application; the next step was to get approval to apply. Requirements were also strict. One had to have a college degree or a viable trade that would qualify them to enter into the US workplace immediately upon arrival. Once an applicant met those requirements, the second big step was to find a sponsor. The sponsor's responsibility to an approved US Immigration Department applicant included the following: Passageway by US troop carrier from Germany to the New York Harbor, secure a paying job reflecting applicant's formal education and/or skills, transportation from New York Harbor to job location, room and board, transportation to and from work and, finally, issuance of $20 in cash upon departure from New York to new job and home destination.

My Uncle began to work with Mr. Wagner. The plan was to send my cousin Frank and me to America first, followed by the remaining family members at a later date.

In late October of that year, I received notice from the American Immigration Bureau that I had been accepted to apply and that I should report to Hanau, near Frankfurt, for consultation to learn about general immigration procedures.

Uncle Martin helped me with these arrangements. The facility in Hanau was an old German army base with complete facilities to accommodate those waiting for their immigration papers to clear. The average stay was about three weeks. General procedure was similar in nature to that of army life—with little to do from day to day until your name was called. Finally, my day came. After my interview and completion of all paperwork, I was told to return home and wait for further confirmation.

In late December, I received notification that my immigration application had been approved and was instructed to return to Hanau by January 25. The joyful news was almost greater than I could bear. However, I was saddened by the fact that Frank declined to go with me as Uncle Martin's business was in financial trouble, and he did not feel free to leave his family under the circumstances.

We all said our goodbyes, and I reported back to Hanau. The excitement grew from day to day while waiting for our ship out of Bremen. In about ten days, word finally came. On February 1, we boarded a train that transported us to the harbor. Our ship was a typical US Army transport carrier by the name of USS General Taylor. I recognized many familiar faces of people who were in the Hanau camp during my first three-week stay. Over the next several days and weeks, I became friends with many of them who remained life-long friends in the US. The majority of all those immigrating to the US at that time were from eastern blocs of Germany, Hungary, Checzoslovacia, Poland, Yugoslavia, Romania and other countries conquered by Communist Russia. We were the lucky ones who escaped these communist hell holes.

Within hours upon arrival at the harbor, we were loaded and the General Taylor troop carrier pulled out of the Port of Bremen into the North Sea, and our ocean voyage to America began.

One Bumpy Ride to Freedom and Opportunity

Never having been on a ship before, it was pretty exciting until England was behind us. Fierce winter ocean storms raged almost all the way to New York. Sea sickness set in on almost all refugees. I was assigned to work in the kitchen until I lost my appetite after three days of the ten-day trip. The rule was: "No work, no eating in the mess hall." I didn't care. It turned out to be a good arrangement on my part. At least I kept my stomach in order and never got seasick again. I ate a candy bar or a sandwich smuggled out of the mess hall by friends on occasion and additionally relied upon the ship's cantina, which was open two hours a day and provided bare essentials for purchase. The German government issued each of us $20 upon departure, so I did have limited alternatives. I spent almost all of my money at the cantina, but it was worth not having to work down below and suffer seasickness the whole trip.

As the ocean storm pounded us most of the trip, I helped friends and acquaintances daily to reach "A" deck for much needed fresh air. "B" deck was mostly used for food preparation and mess hall. The lower decks were sleeping quarters. Bunk beds were mounted on chairs on the aisle side that could be moved for additional living space during the day. With bunks stacked four high, it was particularly a chore for those suffering from sea sickness to reach the top bunks. Some of the elderly looked as white as ghosts. The air down there at times was almost unbearable. I spent most of my time on "A" deck. Although it was cold and icy, orientation and fresh air were very beneficial. Waves were at least three or four stories high. It was truly amazing that no one got washed overboard (that we knew of) with the constant pounding of unbelievable forces of nature.

Oh God, just let us arrive safely. And while you're answering prayers, could you please make it soon? Very soon?

CHAPTER 6

The American Dream

■ ■ ■

THANKS BE TO GOD…WE MADE IT!

AFTER TEN HARROWING DAYS ON the high seas, through a break in the fog, the affirmation I've waited for finally appears: *The Lady* herself—the Statue of Liberty. And what a beautiful sight she is.

The USS General Taylor slowly makes her way to the dock in the New York Harbor. Finally. Safe at last on the shores of America. Standing on the deck watching the ship dock, my whole life seemed to have passed before me at that very moment. I'm one proud immigrant; alive and well, looking forward to my new life living the American dream of freedom and opportunity.

What a relief, and almost in disbelief; I'm safe, and I'm in America. I can't stop saying this over and over to myself. *I'm safe, and I'm in America. I'm in America—I'm in America!!*

Soon after the ship docks, we all begin to unload our old beaten-up suitcases. Many are secured with belts or rope tied around them. Every one of us on the ship is a displaced person who lost everything during the war: our country, our homes, our property and all that was familiar to us, including some family members.

And now comes the moment I have dreamed of. There are no words to express my excitement and pride as I take my first step onto American soil. Like so many others, I get down on my hands and knees and kiss the sidewalk. (Well, surely, there's soil underneath there somewhere.)

To my surprise, I am suddenly surrounded by a swarm of street peddlers speaking *at* me in a language I don't understand. They all display watches up and down both arms and pinned to the lining of their overcoats and wave bags of cheap jewelry and mystery items in my face. Unfortunately for them, I have only just a little over $2.00 on me.

Welcome to America!

Thank goodness, in no time at all, we are met by a German-speaking official who ushers us to a more controlled environment off the street. We're each issued a name tag with numbers and placed in groups according to the location of our final destination. It feels good to just stand on terra firma after that wild ship ride across the ocean. The representative finally calls out,

"Rudolf Seemayer," and with a waving motion summons me to walk toward her. A taxi quickly pulls up. She opens the door, I get in, and she says to the driver,

"Grand Central Station."

Before she closes the door, I inquire, "How long does it take to get to Newark?"

"About thirty minutes," she replied.

"Excuse me, I was told that Newark is approximately three hundred and fifty miles from the harbor."

She looks puzzled for a couple of seconds and, after taking a closer look at my name tag, says,

"Oh my goodness, you are going to **Newark in upstate New York**. I almost sent you to Newark, **New Jersey**."

I'm sure glad I asked. Now my taxi is heading to the Greyhound bus station instead of Grand Central Station. After waiting for about an hour, I finally board the bus at about 9:00 p.m. I figure from the mileage the trip will take approximately eight hours. What I didn't figure on were all the stops the bus made in small towns throughout the trip. Almost nine hours had passed, and I'm getting increasingly uneasy. Unable to speak or understand English, every time the bus stopped and the bus driver made an announcement; I'd jump up and ask;

"Nevark?" (German pronunciation of Newark)

Each time, the bus driver waved his hand and shook his head *no, not yet* as if to say, I'll let you know. Although I am pretty sure he won't forget me, I'm getting very anxious by now and can't keep from jumping up at every stop and repeating the same question. After a very long twelve-hour ride, I'm awakened by the hand of the bus driver gently shaking me on the shoulder, saying in a rather quiet voice,

"Nevark."

I jump up, gathering my old suitcase and overcoat, and scurry toward the door. As I take my first step down the exit, I turn and look back at the bus driver to wave and thank him. With a nice smile, tipping his head slowly in an approving sort of way, he waves goodbye to me as if to say,

"Good luck, young man, welcome to America."

Welcome Home – to America

Just as I step off the bus, a very nice lady, Mrs. Spolteholtz, who turns out to be a co-owner of Wayne Country Floral, my new employer, greets me in German and escorts me to my new home riding in her large American luxury car. We engage in small talk on the way, while the whole time I'm thinking; *I'm in America in the presence of really nice German-speaking lady who just happens to own a beautiful American luxury car. If only my Uncle Martin and family could see me now.*

The home I was assigned to live in belonged to another German-speaking lady by the name of Mrs. Scheetz. Room and board, which included rent, three meals a day, seven days a week plus laundry services cost a whopping $10.00 per week.

Mrs. Scheetz gave me a very warm welcome and helped me get settled into my nice big room with lots of windows dressed in beautiful European type curtains. I felt at home already. That bed sure looked good. By this time I felt totally exhausted and could hardly keep my eyes open. Thank goodness, I was left to sleep almost the whole day, interrupted only a couple of times by a knock on my door with the delivery of a wonderful meal Mrs. Scheetz prepared for me.

After one day's rest, it's time to go to work. I awaken early, anxious and excited to get to my new job and meet everyone. After eating a big breakfast, my landlord's son drops me off at work.

Owners of Wayne Floral Company were the Mohrs', originally from northern Germany, and the Spaldeholtzs': Mr. Spaldeholtz from Holland and Mrs. Spaldeholtz from Vienna.

Everyone at work was very friendly and helpful to me in every way. One of the owner's sons, Heinz, spoke very good German. My life was made much easier and more pleasant by his friendship and ability to translate, as my English was nonexistent in the beginning. Within a short time, I enroll in night school to learn and practice speaking English.

Wayne Floral specialized in growing chrysanthemum cuttings and fully developed flowers which were shipped to wholesalers throughout New York State.

I adapted very quickly to the American way of life, including the love of cars, dollars and clothing. I stayed in close contact with my family in Germany and sent as many nylons by mail as I could afford. Nylons (stockings) at that time in Germany were a very valuable commodity used for trading on the black market in exchange for food and other needed items.

After approximately eight months, I saved enough money to buy a 1942 Pontiac for $350.00 that had an engine from "here to there." It ran like a top, and I felt like a million dollars sitting behind the wheel in this big American car. After all, a car was a must, especially for dating. My friend Heinz had chauffeured me around long enough. We double dated a lot, and I met many of his college buddies who all seemed to come from wealthy families. I also met some of the parents of these guys who owned factories. They all accepted and treated me as a member of their family. This was definitely unlike Germany, where company owners and officials did not, as a rule, mingle socially with "working class" individuals. It felt good to be respected and accepted. Everyone wanted to help me any way they could. All the great things I heard about living in America were true! And now, America is *my* home.

When I was ready to take my driver's license test, Heinz let me use his car, which had an automatic shift. His mother, Mrs. Mohr, drove me to the court house for the test. I was still working on my English reading and speaking skills in night school, so the officer was kind enough to give me an oral exam. Aware of this ahead of time, Mrs. Mohr and I came to somewhat of an *understanding* before we arrived for the test. It was decided she would sit in the back seat and, when the officer read the true or false question, if I hesitated, she would cough or clear her throat quietly for a "true" answer or remain silent for the "false." I wanted that driver's license. After all, I had only been in the US for eight months and had already saved enough money to pay cash for my very own car. Now, all I needed was a driver's license—otherwise, I'd find myself continuing to sit in the driveway behind the wheel going nowhere. In looking back, I have to laugh realizing the officer surely must have caught on to our little "trick" after about the third question he read aloud. I thought to myself at the time, anyone would have to be a total loser not to love this country! I passed the test. Well, to be a bit more honest, Mrs. Mohr and I passed the test. Thanks, Mrs. Mohr.

Finally, I was independent. It was me, my car and the open road. Now I could go visit friends I made on the ship who settled in nearby Buffalo and in New York City. Man, it didn't get any better than this. All my hard work in school paid off, allowing passageway and opportunity to come to America with a nice job waiting for me, nice people to work with, a wonderful place to live, money in my pocket, a community of friends and acquaintances always ready to help me in any way and, now, my very own car in my name with freedom to go anywhere I pleased. No doubt, I was living the great American dream.

Top priority on my visitation list was my sponsor, Mr. Wagner, who lived in Brooklyn. I never met the man, as my uncle made all the arrangements with him on my behalf in Frankfurt. Mr. Wagner was pleasantly surprised to see me and showed me around his knitting factory. Naturally, the purpose of my visit was to meet and personally thank him for the great opportunity he gave me to come to America and all else he did for me. He seemed genuinely proud of the accomplishments I had made in a short time and, upon my departure, wished me continued good luck. I proceed on with my journey, visiting other friends in the area, and made the best of my time seeing the sights in and around New York City.

I often made weekend trips to nearby Buffalo to visit the Witt family I met on the ship coming over. Even though we always got around to talking about hard times and the loss of those who didn't make it out or were never heard from again, we always celebrated our new life in America with happiness, joy and gratitude.

CHAPTER 7

The Soldier's Life in Germany

■ ■ ■

1953

"Greetings," the letter began. After being in the US for about a year, I received a formal *invitation* from Uncle Sam to report for active duty. After some discussion with my friend Heinz, I replied with a letter written in German, along with the English translation attached, telling them I was still studying English in night school.

Six months later, a second *invitation* arrived, and I was drafted in to the US Army. My induction papers were issued in November of 1953. I was sent to Camp Kilmer in New Jersey. Two days after processing, we flew to Columbia, South Carolina, to Fort Jackson for basic training. Upon arrival, it didn't take long to realize my English still needed a lot of improvement. At first, I thought the drill instructors were speaking another language, but it was explained to me that it was the Deep South accent that had me confused. I quickly learned to just follow along and fall in line with whatever the other troops were doing to avoid needless punishment such as pushups.

The next sixteen weeks of basic training are both interesting and enjoyable. After working manual labor in the greenhouses, I am in excellent physical condition, and I have no problem with discipline. And besides, I'm finally getting to live my dream. I am an American soldier.

After eight weeks of basic training, we are given a ten-day pass. I hop a train and head for Newark to visit friends and to pick up my car. The visit was great, but I was anxious to get out on the open road in my car and get back to base. I stopped in Buffalo and picked up a couple other guys who rode back with me. This is just another installment of living the American dream.

I'm now a US soldier seeing America in my own car. Life was good.

Back at camp and basic training in Fort Jackson, Pvt. James E. Carson, editor of the 61st Infantry Regiment post newspaper, *The Hilltopper*, asked to interview me. He was interested in where I came from, how I came to America and how I ended up serving in the US Army. He was quite surprised that I had only been in the US for a short time—not a citizen—and yet, I was drafted into the US Armed Forces. I relayed several stories about my experiences during and after the war as a young boy, a refugee and a *displaced person,* and how the US Army came to our rescue when there was little hope for our survival and safety. I told him of my dream to, one day, become one of "them." At the end of the interview, he asked,

"Would you like to become a citizen?"

"Yes," I answered. "That's why I'm here."

This was my opportunity to further my case.

"My big hope is that somehow, because of my service in the US Army, there might be an exception to the normal five-year eligibility waiting period rule before applying for citizenship."

Not long after that interview, the editor began working on my behalf. He sent a copy of his article, along with a request for "Waiver of Time Limits for Citizenship Application," to the company commander. Astonishingly, within five weeks of that interview two other soldiers of German descent, a Nigerian and I received great news: we had a special invitation from Augusta, Georgia, to be sworn in as American citizens! I could not believe what I was reading. Maybe my English had failed me—again. Maybe I wasn't reading it right. Maybe it was some kind of joke. I still wasn't sure of what I was reading until several of my buddies read it and assured me it was a valid formal invitation to be sworn in as an American citizen. What an incredible surprise! I just kept thinking about Uncle Martin who had the wisdom and foresight to prepare me for immigration from war-torn Germany to America.

Orders were signed, and the four of us were issued a thirty-six hour pass. Off we went in my 1942 straight eight Pontiac on our five-hour drive to Augusta. We couldn't get there fast enough. As we entered Georgia, my limousine was making great time. Excitement grew until I spotted the flashing lights of a state trooper's vehicle in my rearview mirror.

I pull over. Dressed in full uniform, we all get out and hand our identification to the trooper. He takes his own sweet time looking over our papers then, in a stern deep voice, asks,

"Did you realize you were speeding through two counties and several towns?"

"No Sir, I didn't realize that, Sir!" (In typical respectful Army style)

"So what's the big hurry?" he asked.

In unison, as if rehearsed, we all reach for our special invitations and proudly show to him. His demeanor immediately changes. A big smile replaces that once stern look on his face, and his eyes soften. He shakes our hands, congratulates each of us and sends us on our way, but not before he hands me a warning ticket.

We arrive in Augusta around 7:00 p.m. and check into a cheap hotel near the courthouse. The lock on the outside door was broken, so we blocked the door closed with a dresser. We had a big laugh over this place.

At eight o'clock the next morning, we were all spit-shined, excited and ready to go. After breakfast and a quick sightseeing tour of the town, we report to the courthouse at 9:45 sharp. This place was jammed with about 150 immigrants from all over the world. The entire proceedings lasted only about thirty minutes. After the final swearing in ceremony was over, we all congratulated one another, feeling very fortunate and lucky to now be American citizens. It was time to head back to the base. It sure felt good returning to the base as a proud US citizen.

The Last Train Out

The last half of basic training was almost over. This meant duty assignment locations would soon be made. I inquired about the possibility of getting an overseas assignment and was told those assignments were issued to fewer than ten of the most *elite* soldiers out of the whole company. Although I didn't understand the meaning of *elite*, I did understand that some assignments would be made, and my name should be one of them. So I was granted a meeting with the company commander and the base chaplain. I briefly told them about some of the challenges my relatives and I faced during and after the war, how I came to the US and how much it would mean to have the opportunity to return to Germany and visit those relatives; to show them, with their help, I was now living my big dream as an American citizen serving in the US Army.

I made notes before the meeting to make sure I said anything and everything that might influence a decision to get my name on that list. When neither of them seemed to even be listening, I closed my presentation and thanked them for their time. I was told bluntly that I had come to the wrong place, to the wrong people—that they had no influence or authority whatsoever to make such a request on my behalf. I felt pretty let down and sad.

Within the next few days, an inspection was called. It was announced that one person out of the Company would be selected as Colonel's orderly. I didn't have a clue what that meant. It seemed we stood at attention forever while the company commander paraded back and forth among the ranks and files inspecting each soldier, seeming to make marks by each of our names. After the inspection, he turned and consulted with a couple of other "brass" then faced us and spoke.

"Pvt. 1st Class Rudolf Seemayer, please step forward." I guess I would have been excited if I actually knew what being selected as "Colonel's orderly" actually meant. It must have been something good to make all that fuss over.

Later that afternoon, I was summoned to the company commander's office, given instructions on my duties as Colonel's orderly, and then was issued white gloves, white strings for my boots and a white helmet to wear with my regular uniform on special assignment with the Colonel.

The next morning, right on time, I am presented to the Colonel. As I accompany him during inspections of various training site areas, the old guy strikes up a conversation with me. He immediately detects my broken English and accent and begins asking me questions like,

"Where are you from—how did you come to the US, and how do you like the Army?" and so on.

He seemed genuinely interested and intrigued by my story. I proceeded to give him about the same story I gave the company commander and chaplain, except, this time my audience of one was interested, and I felt motivated and comfortable telling the whole story. He was a very good listener and wanted to hear more. At the end of our day together, he asked me one last question,

"If you could do anything you wanted right now, what would it be?"

Without hesitation, I answered;

"To return to Germany and visit my relatives as an American citizen serving in the United States Army." He smiled, shook my hand and then thanked me for my service that day and for my continued service to *our* country. It was quite an extraordinary experience. I felt honored.

A few days after basic training was completed, our company was ordered outside for roll call. All at attention, the company commander proceeded to tell us he would be reading the names of those selected for overseas duty. As he went down the alphabet calling out a few names, the "S's" drew closer and closer. My heart was pounding. I thought for sure it was going to jump right out of my chest. Although my earlier appeal to that same company commander seemed to have fallen on deaf ear, somehow, I still held out hope. The commander seemed to just drag the process out, looking down, flipping back and forth through the list of names on his clipboard. As he raised his head to speak, I held my breath and may have even closed my eyes. Waiting. There were two hundred and twenty soldiers in my company, and less than ten would get the nod. I never did find out what *elite* meant. What are the odds? One name in the S's was called and in correct alphabetical order, my name would be next. It was now or never for me. I'm pretty sure I stopped breathing. And then in a bold voice, the company commander barked out quite loudly,

"Private 1st Class Rudolf Seemayer, report for European duty at 0800." As I started to breathe again a million things went through my mind at that very moment: my family, the war, my escape, my mother and a series of events that brought me to this very moment!

There was a big celebration right there on the field once we were dismissed. The company commander walked toward me with a big smile on his face. His eyes softened as he saluted then stuck his hand out for a hand shake. He offered his congratulations and wished me luck finding my family in Germany.

I'll never know exactly how my name got placed on that list, but, maybe, just maybe my company commander and the chaplain were listening after all. And might there have been some collaboration between them and the old Colonel on my behalf?

I guess this means I'm among the eight *elite* soldiers now. I'm still not sure exactly what it means, but I think it's something really good. Elite or not, I'm one happy and grateful soul; I'm going back to Germany as an American citizen serving *my* country in the US Army. I can't wait to see my relatives.

"Hello, Aunt Tillie, It's Me, Rudi"
May 1954

Camp Kilmer, New Jersey, was one of the major staging areas for troops being transported to and from Europe. While waiting on the carrier to arrive and deployment papers to be processed, the eight of us join all the others in briefings and classes to learn about overseas duties and protocol for serving in a foreign country. Two days prior to departure, our new papers are issued. The name on the envelope read: **Rudolph Seamayer**. This seems to be my name, but something's not right. I approach the clerk at the desk and bring to his attention that my name is misspelled. Without hesitation, he looks straight at me and replies,

"It could take several weeks to get this correction done. If you want to be on that ship headed to Germany in two days, you are now **R u d o l p h S e a m a y e r**" as he spelled out each letter of my name.

"Yes sir! Not a problem." I figured changing the spelling of my name was but a small price to pay for all the privilege I had been given.

Then we finally load and leave New Jersey for Germany. It was truly like a vacation made in heaven for me. Since I had already made this ocean trip in January of 1952, I braced myself for the worst and gave fair warning to all the "first timers." However, we soon learn that weather conditions between May and October are generally ideal for sailing. The seven-day cruise was an incredibly pleasant experience for us all.

Upon arrival in Bremerhafen, (northern Germany near Bremen), assignments were issued and troops loaded on trains headed for various locations across Germany. I was assigned to the base in Gelenhausen. As soon as I arrive at the base that afternoon, I call my relatives who live in Stuttgart right away.

"Hello."

"Is this Aunt Tillie?"

"Yes, it's Tillie. Who is this?"

"It's Rudy...your nephew, Rudy."

There was silence for a few seconds and still, with some doubt in her voice, she repeated,

"Rudy? Rudy Seamayer?"

"Yes, it's me, and I'm in Gelenhausen."

"I don't believe it's you; why are you in Gelenhausen? When did you get here? Anne, it's your cousin Rudy, and he's in Germany, in Gelenhausen!"

"Can all of you come to Gelenhausen to see me today or tomorrow?" I asked.

"Your Uncle Martin and Frank are out of town on a business trip and can't be reached. I'm not sure Anne and I should come without contacting Martin," she replied.

When they finally made contact with Uncle Martin, she reported back to me that he suggested they wait until the following weekend to come see me.

But I just *have* to see them—*now*. I must figure out a way to make it happen. Maybe, if I tell them there's a possibility I'll be shipped to France right away, they'll come. Sure enough, the little white lie worked. They said they'd come—now.

While they were in route, I went to the command post and asked for a six-hour pass. I was told that no passes were issued to new soldiers until their week-long orientation was completed. I asked to see the company commander. I explained my story and told him my family from Stuttgart was already on their way. He made an exception and issued me a six-hour pass.

Within a few hours, Aunt Tillie and Cousin Anne arrived at the base. What a reunion it was. We all hugged, laughed and cried; so happy to see one another again. We made the best of my six-hour pass. Aunt Tillie just kept saying,

"Wait until your Uncle Martin and Frank see you in your US Army uniform."

It was really great seeing them. We talked about so many things. I thought my Aunt Tillie (my mother's sister) might have heard something definite about my mother, but, sadly, there was no news. My time was up, we said our goodbyes and they headed back home.

Soon, I got to go to Stuttgart and see the whole family. My Uncle Martin, indeed, was so very proud of me. It was great having the opportunity to thank him for all he and the whole family did for me. Naturally, they wanted to know every detail about my life in the US, about my job, about getting my citizenship, how I came to serve in the US Army and how I got the assignment to serve my time in Germany. My visits with family in Stuttgart were a monthly occurrence. I also had the opportunity to visit with family who ended up in Vienna, Austria, after the war. The eighteen months of duty in Germany were some of the best times of my life.

Our regimental base of the 12th Infantry 4th Division in Gelenhausen was newly constructed. Each company was housed in one building with four floors. The base was within walking distance of the town and, of course, we made the best of our free time. However, we also had a great time catching a train to nearby Frankfurt where the action never stopped. (Locals often found it fascinating that someone wearing a US Army uniform could speak such perfect German.)

One of my best friends in our platoon in Gelenhausen was Bruno Romej, also of German descent. Bruno and I had a great time together, on and off the base. He was only nineteen years old but very sharp and disciplined. He always tried to beat me out of Colonel's orderly whenever possible. I was glad to finally learn that being chosen a Colonel's orderly was, indeed, a good thing. Whenever a company had to pull guard duty on post, one man was selected for Colonel's orderly for that day. The big payoff of getting selected for this job was an automatic three-day pass from the Colonel as well as an extra three-day pass from the company commander.

Army days in Germany

After about four months of good times and fun, I was recommended for an eight-week cycle Non Commissioned Officers Training School. We were housed at an offbeat resort type complex that was absolutely beautiful. The problem was we didn't have much time to enjoy the surroundings as school started at 7:30 in the morning and lasted until 5:00 in the afternoon, five days a week. In addition, there was plenty of homework to keep us busy on weekends. The biggest problem I encountered at this school was my lack of reading and writing skills in English. Fortunately, my roommate was a great help tutoring me outside the classroom.

After the first four-week cycle, we were allowed to go on leave for the weekend; however, we were warned it was easy to fall behind if all we did all weekend was party. The majority of us decided to split for the weekend to have a little fun for a change. When I returned, I paid big time for that little weekend of fun. I fell way behind, even though I stayed up many nights until 2:00 a.m. studying. I was glad to make it through that course. When our eight weeks were finished, we were transported back to base in Gelenhausen and given our last standard testing for night tactical assault. I passed, was promoted to Corporal and received my extra strip along with a whopping $15.00 per month raise. Considering a fair meal at a restaurant cost only about a dollar, the extra money came in handy.

After duty in Gelenhausen, I was transferred to Aschaffenburg. The base there was an old German army base. Each room housed one to three men. I was assigned to a room with two other guys. Our building faced street side, giving us opportunities to talk to the fraulines without leaving the base. We had it made.

It didn't take us long to find *the* hot spot in downtown Aschaffenburg: The Dixie Bar, with live music and plenty of fraulines to enjoy. The spiral staircase coming down from the upstairs bar was the talk of the town. The glass door at the bottom of the staircase got broken at least once a week by some drunken fool slipping and falling down the stairs, crashing into the front door.

Two weeks after my arrival in Aschaffenburg, I heard a rumor that our regiment was seeking soccer players to form a team. I was lucky enough to make the team along with many other players from all over Europe who immigrated to the US and were now serving in the US Army. We practiced every afternoon and had games scheduled every weekend while the other troops were on maneuvers. Life was good.

One morning, orders came to send all the able-bodied men to the maneuver grounds. I loaded my gear, and off I went. When I reported to my company someone asked,

"What are you doing here? Your soccer team just left for the base."

After I was told there was no available transportation for the next two or three days back to base, I decided to call the motor pool for help. They said they'd let me know if there was a truck going back the next morning. I was not very optimistic by what I heard. The next morning at 8:00 a.m. the platoon met at the designated staging area with enough gear and weapons to last a week in the field. Just as we started to pull out, to my surprise, my name was called and I was given orders to join up with my soccer team back at the base. I was all too happy to unload all my heavy gear and catch my ride back to base. Playing on the soccer team, traveling and competing was an incredible experience. The team eventually dissolved due to transfers resulting in a lack of players. But it was great fun while it lasted.

Not long after that, one morning in regular formation, our master sergeant asked for volunteers for an undisclosed duty or "detail." He only revealed to us that qualified men would not be sorry. It sounded interesting, so I volunteered. After breakfast the next morning, a certain number of volunteers were chosen. We still did not know any details about the mission.

When we arrived at headquarters, we were taken to a meeting room and addressed by a Major. The Major informed us that the regiment was forming a shooting team and that eighteen of the best shooters would be selected out of the group of volunteers to compete in pistols, rifles and B.A.R. competition against other regiments and, eventually, against all divisions stationed in Europe. After several weeks of training, I qualified for the eight-man B.A.R. team. The remainder of the team consisted of an eight-man rifle team and a two-man 45 caliber pistol team. Military rank in this shooting team meant nothing as these sharp shooters ranked from PFC to Major. Our shooting team lasted for about three months with lots of good times. During this time, our team was exempt from all duties, including maneuvers. We became the best shots in the First Division after a period of training. Our daily schedule began with breakfast at 7:00 a.m., load the truck at 8:00 and head for the range for shooting practice until around noon. Then it was back to base for lunch, weapons cleaning in the afternoon then get ready to pick up our pass and head for town in the evening. Talk about the "life of Riley"—he never had it so good. The fun finally ended with the final divisional competition "shootout" in which our team finished third of the five American Divisions.

My overall routine and activities while stationed in Germany was such an incredibly pleasant situation, I often thought about signing up for lifetime duty. However, there was always a shortage of money in the service, and I knew this would not be a suitable life for me.

The black market trade was basically nonexistent in the mid-'50s as goods were plentiful to the civilian population. The only GIs making extra big bucks were either loan sharks or guys stealing and selling government supplies. Our company had such a guy. He loaned money for 100% interest. When payday came, he had his "strong arms" all over the regiment collecting outstanding loans at the exit door of the pay buildings. That Corporal made more money than the top company commander, calculating his income somewhere between $3–5,000.00 per month. Needless to say, he was a career man and had no desire or motivation to leave the service. He had one shrewd illegal operation going. He loaned money to as many officers as possible so no one complained. Others got rich off stealing and selling US Army officers' overcoats. Once, on a return trip to our regimental base, our truck suddenly stopped and unloaded two large bundles of officers' overcoats. The transaction took place right there in broad daylight with German civilians. I'm sure these were not the only US Army-issued goods being stolen and sold to locals.

Beautiful Vienna, Austria
August 1955

In mid-August, I picked up my last two-week pass. In full US Army uniform, I caught a train headed for Vienna, Austria to visit Uncle Julius, Aunt Elizabeth, Cousin Tilde and other friends and relatives.

Vienna is still occupied by the *big four*: the Americans, British, French and Russians. It is understood that allied soldiers are subject to harassment and even arrest and detainment in the Russian zones in both Vienna and Berlin. Upon the advice of our company commander, I was to head straight to the GI center at the rail station as soon as I arrived in Vienna. I entered and identified myself.

"I am in Vienna for several days to visit relatives. Can you please advise me of any local travel directives or warnings about the city and, in particular, the Russian zone?"

He picked up a long pointer or baton and walked toward a giant city map of Vienna that hung on the wall.

"It is safe to travel about Vienna with the exception of the Russian Zone, which is located across the Danube River Bridge," he tapped multiple times on the exact location of the bridge with his pointer. He continued;

"GIs who cross into this zone are highly subject to harassment and even arrest and detainment without grounds or merit. It is recommended travel into this area be avoided altogether."

I thank him for the information then ask if he can help me find directions to my relative's house on the big map. He can't find the address. I leave. As I step out of the station onto the street, I approach a lady passing by. Speaking in German, I ask if she can help me find *this* particular address, as I show her the piece of paper it's written on. She takes the paper from my hand, is silent for several seconds as she seems to study it, and then begins giving me specific directions and instructions: which street car to catch, its location, where to exit and walking directions from there. I'm in luck! She is both surprised and complimentary (and a bit confused with my US Army uniform on) about how well I speak the language.

I thank her, grab my suitcase, walk to the next block as directed, jump on my designated streetcar, locate a good seat, relax and begin to enjoy the scenery. Within about ten minutes, I suddenly realize we are on the Danube River Bridge—and we're crossing over to the Russian zone. And here I am in full Army uniform.

Either the lady's directions are wrong, or my relatives live in the Russian zone. I suddenly feel very anxious and even fearful given all the warnings about crossing over into this area. I talk to myself,

"Stop! Reason things out. I'm already here, so hopefully the address exists in this area and I can find it before I'm spotted by a Russian soldier on patrol. Stay focused. Stay positive…just get off the train and follow the directions."

I felt some relief when I recognized the street name of my exit was next. As I step off the streetcar, I look back and spot two Russian soldiers exiting the same streetcar I was on about three cars back. They begin to walk my way. My heart is pounding as I walk a bit faster and faster toward my relative's address. Are they following me? Am I going to get arrested? After all, I am an American soldier in full uniform, easy to spot. They are still walking behind me after about three blocks. According to the directions, at the end of this block, I turn left. Thank goodness, they turn right. I breathe a little easier now. Another close call.

The lady's directions were perfect. After a couple more turns, I finally arrived safely at my relative's house. Knock. Knock. Knock. No one answers the door. I knock a couple more times and wait, but still no answer. Maybe the door is unlocked. I turn the knob and walk right into the kitchen where my Uncle Julius is sitting at the table reading the newspaper. I didn't want to startle him so I quietly called out his name,

"Uncle Julius? Uncle *Julius?*"

He turns around and, in total disbelief, slowly gets to his feet. We hug and cry of happiness to see one another. He grabbed my shoulders and held me away from him at arm's length (I think to make sure his eyes were not deceiving him) then we'd hug again. This went on three or four times until he was convinced it was *me*, and I was really *there*. He kept repeating, "Rudy, it's you, and an American soldier. Just look at you, you made it—an American soldier."

The reunion was a particularly emotional one since the last time we saw one another was October 1, 1944, in Werschetz when he picked my mother and me up with his horse and buggy and took us to the train station to catch The Last Train Out.

Aunt Elizabeth made us a nice meal. We sat at the table for two or three hours talking about those earlier days. He had lots of questions. I told him about the troubles we had after we left Werschetz by train, how things were for us during and after the war, how I met up and lived with Hilde and all about her death, about my going to live with Uncle Martin and Aunt Tillie, about my schooling and about my immigration to the US.

Uncle Julius and my mother were sister and brother. They were very close and, therefore, all we kids spent a lot of good times together. After my father died when I was only eleven years old, Uncle Julius quickly became a loving father figure to me. Our visit conjured up a lot of memories and events we all experienced in those earlier days, including the decision my mother had to make to allow me to flee Yugoslavia.

As the Russians moved closer and closer to invading our town, every parent of children of a certain age had to make the decision of whether to allow their children to leave by train to, hopefully, a safer environment. Uncle Julius was there by my mother's side to encourage and help her realize that I'd have a better chance for survival if I were allowed to flee by train with the others. He had the tough job of also pointing out the serious consequences of how things might end up for all Germans remaining behind when the Russians moved in. Because of this madman Hitler, anyone of German descent was in grave danger and considered the enemy, no matter what country they lived in and no matter whether they were a child or an adult. If they were German, they were automatically considered the enemy.

As a parent now, I can understand what a hard decision it must have been for my mother to allow me to leave, not knowing if she'd ever see me again or what circumstance or dangers we might encounter along the escape route to safety.

He went back through the whole story and remembered every detail. I'm sure he must have been quite apprehensive about the whole situation, but he never let it show. In fact, after my mother and I were in the buggy and my last bag was loaded, he laughed and let out with a big modern day "High-Ho-Silver" and off we went to the train station.

As we continued to visit, Aunt Elizabeth looked at the clock and told me Tilde would be home from work soon. And soon, in she walks.

"Surprise!" we all yell out.

Oh, what a reunion that was with more tears, more celebrating and more stories. The last time I saw Tilde was in 1948 in Germany when she was released from Russian prison work camp. Her brother, Ferdinand, was shot to death on the Yugoslavia border as he tried to escape into Romania. It's amazing how much one can endure and somewhere deep inside find the courage and the will to carry on.

During the next three days, I spent time with my relatives and school buddies, many of whom I hadn't seen since we all fled Werschetz in 1944. They took me all around the city and showed me off in uniform with cameras clicking at every beautiful sight in Vienna.

Sightseeing in Vienna with Hilde, Rudigard and friends

On that third day of sightseeing, Tilde and I were invited by one of my long-time childhood friends and neighbor from Werschetz to a garden restaurant where an orchestra and the famous Caterina Valente were performing. Tilde insisted I wear my uniform. We were having a great time. As we all visit around our table, a fellow sitting at the next table dressed in civilian clothes overheard our conversation about my staying in the Russian sector. It so happens he was an M.P. American GI of German descent, stationed in West Berlin on holiday in Vienna enjoying himself. We visit for a while and then he offers me some good advice.

"Since you are in uniform, I would suggest your cousin take a streetcar and go home by herself, and you catch a ride with someone who will drive you directly home in order to arrive undetected." We took his advice and both made it home safely. For the remainder of my stay, I decided to play it safe and dress in civilian clothes.

What an incredible visit it was spending time with friends and relatives, especially considering all we went through during and after the war.

I was in hopes my uncle or other relatives might have found out what happened to my mom, but rumors and hearsay are all we ever had to go on.

In October that same year, all occupied troops of the big four powers pulled out of Vienna, and the city and country of Austria were free and independent once again.

Farewell to Family

I said farewell to my relatives and friends in Vienna and boarded a train for Stuttgart, Germany, to catch up with Aunt Tillie, Uncle Martin, Anne and Frank. For the next several days, we had a great time visiting and just being together. I caught them up on all the family news from Vienna and learned what had been going on with my uncle's family (the Hubers) in Stuttgart. Naturally, they wanted to know more about my experiences in the US.

It was really great fun and good to have the opportunity to visit with family before shipping back to the US. They were all so happy for me and proud I was serving in the US Army and now a US citizen. During this time spent with family, I was able to find a lot of pieces to a giant puzzle about family history during and after the war that had been missing for a long time. But the one thing still missing is how and when my mother died. But now, after talking with all my relatives face to face in Germany and Austria, I'll do my best to lay it to rest...to accept that I'll probably never know. Many of my relatives made it to safety before the Russians moved in. I always hoped my mother might have been one of them.

After an incredible vacation visiting with family and friends, I returned to the base in Aschaffenburg. Within two weeks, I was reporting to the general hospital in Frankfurt for a tonsillectomy. The hospital was constantly overcrowded and, unless one had a life-threatening illness or serious emergency, appointments had to be made two or three months in advance. My master sergeant was not happy about all my time off and wanted me to cancel my operation. But it was not for him to decide.

Three days after my operation, I returned to base with a sore throat and still unable to swallow. I thought it would be nice to recuperate back in Stuttgart for a few days. I knew my Aunt Tillie would prepare soft food for me and maybe even serve me ice cream. I was not in the mood to go on maneuvers and, besides, to my knowledge release papers had not been signed at the hospital. For the next few days, Aunt Tillie showered me with tender loving care just as my mother would have done. It was a wonderful few days. Thank God for Aunt Tillie.

When I finally returned to base with hospital discharge papers in hand, there was only a skeleton crew of new officials on hand. No one even knew I had been gone.

RETURN TO THE USA

We had plenty of leisure time to pack to get ready for the trip back to the US. We said goodbye to all the fraulines and friends we made. It was time to go. Approximately five companies loaded onto troop carriers. Two companies were selected for either guard duty or kitchen patrol. Luckily, my company was chosen for guard duty.

I have mixed emotions about leaving Germany and my family; however, with my military service nearing an end, it's exciting to think about new life adventures and the pursuit of personal and professional fulfillment as a citizen of the United States of America.

Saying goodbye to Germany

CHAPTER 8

At Home In America

■ ■ ■

OCTOBER 1955

AFTER SIX DAYS AT SEA, we sail into the New York Harbor. The sight of Lady Liberty this time takes on a whole new meaning, as now America is *my* country, and I'm privileged to enjoy all the freedom and opportunity she has to offer.

We disembark and are immediately transferred to Camp Kilmer, New Jersey. Two days later, my discharge papers were processed. Goodbye US Army. Hello new life in America. I head for New York City. Walking around the city, a US citizen, with over $800.00 muster out pay in my pocket and no responsibilities at the moment, I'm feeling free as a bird. I stop into a restaurant, have a nice meal, and with nothing to do or no place to go, I leisurely get up and stroll outside. As I stand gazing at the deli's showcase outside the restaurant, I feel a big (and firm) hand on my shoulder. A booming voice addresses me,

"Is that the way you eat around the City, without paying?"

As I turn to go back inside the restaurant, I apologize and try to explain to him that I just forgot to pay. I lay a $10 bill down on the counter. As he makes change, he continues to complain and tell me he could have me arrested. I take my change and waste no time getting out of there.

It was really great meeting up with friends and enjoying the sights and sounds of the City for the next few days, but now it's time to think about my future. I have to admit, it's a bit scary but also very exciting to now have the opportunity to pursue my own *American dream*.

I keep hearing all these fantastic success stories about careers in sales. US factories that once produced war materials are now producing all sorts of consumer goods, creating a need for sales personnel to promote and sell their products. But, realistically, I know I need more work on my English speaking skills to make this happen.

I always remember when I left for the service, Mr. Mohr told me I could always come back to work for him at the nursery in Newark. I knew it would be a matter of time before I found the job of my dreams in sales but, meanwhile, I'd work for Mr. Mohr. After all, he gave me my start when I first arrived in the US in February of 1952 as a displaced person. Once again, he came through offering me a job paying $1.25 per hour, the same rate his younger son was earning. It was a great place to work until my dream job came through at some point. I'm forever grateful to the Mohrs for their kindness, friendship and support shown to me through the years.

Not long after I begin working for the Mohrs, I get an invitation to attend a sales meeting from one of my friends who lives in Buffalo. He convinces me that almost all of their salesmen drive new Cadillacs. Who could turn down an offer like that? It sounded good to me, so I agreed to attend the meeting. The product turned out to be vacuum cleaners manufactured in Anaheim, California. The product was good and impressive but, priced at $340 per unit, it was a tough sell. However, I couldn't erase that picture in my mind of me sitting behind the wheel of that new Cadillac so I signed up to participate in two home demonstrations.

On the first sales call, I immediately developed a negative attitude when the salesman tossed up two ping pong balls and caught them one by one in mid-air, demonstrating the strength of the suction. This was not exactly what I had in mind. But, being new to all of this, the Cadillac promise gave me reason to at least try it. I lasted less than a week and didn't sell one unit. That job *sucked*.

Once again, Mr. Mohr put me back to work. Good old Mr. Mohr. He never gave up on me. He knew I had big ideas and dreams of continuing to better myself. He was supportive of anything I wanted to try. He'd always say,

"If this doesn't work out, you know you always have a job here."

One night at a local bar in Newark, I met a gentleman by the name of Ed Anders. I became very good friends with him and his wife Myrtle who were friends with a lot of affluent and influential people in the area. When they found out I wanted to develop a career in sales, they insisted on introducing me to a friend of theirs who was the retired president of C.W. Stewart Company in Palmyra, New York. At that time, C.W. Stewart was one of the largest direct sales organizations in the country, which included five nursery companies, two jewelry companies and a cosmetic company. Within a few days, I met with his friend for an interview. Even though my English still needed some work, he convinced me that if I knew how to grow plants then I could learn to sell them. Next was a meeting with the district manager, Norm Roblee. Norm and I got along great. Once again, I quit my job at the Mohrs and began canvassing up and down streets in Rochester where Norm lived. The object was to get an appointment in the morning, then return one evening that same week to present a landscape design and plan.

The company's canned sales pitch was about four pages long. When I make my first call with one of the more experienced company salesmen, I ring the doorbell, a lady comes to the door and I make the introductions. Without giving her a chance to speak, I proceeded to quote the sales pitch—word for word. She listened politely throughout the whole thing and, when I finish, she asks,

"Could you please repeat that? I didn't quite understand everything you said."

Could it have been my thick German accent? Or did she just get bored and stop listening somewhere along the way, too polite to cut me off? I'm sure it was a bit of both. The salesman I was with couldn't believe I quoted the whole thing from memory! We have a good laugh as he explains that the four-page presentation is only to be used as a guide to extract specific talking points.

"Just speak to potential customers in a personal and friendly way when telling them about our products and services."

His advice sure worked. After striking out on that first disastrous house call, I book three appointments that same morning.

Once an appointment is booked, we then measure the perimeter of the house and yard, draw up a custom landscape plan that includes evergreens and coloring shrubs for year-round beauty and return that same week for the presentation.

In no time, I made the "$1,000 Club" in sales per week, earning a whopping 25% commission. This sales business is even better than I ever dreamed. I feel so confident that I decide to visit my friends in Brooklyn and then canvas new homes on Long Island. After three days' work, I come up empty handed. But all is not lost. I hit the beach every afternoon and really enjoy myself.

I was now making around $800 a month and soon got the new car fever. Norm encouraged me to go ahead with my plan and buy that Crown Victoria convertible I wanted so bad, as he was sure I would continue to prosper. You know what? He was right. Not only was I enjoying success in my dream job, but this kind of personal contact sale proved to be a perfect opportunity to meet some of the nicest most generous people one could ever imagine. Some even offered me jobs. Detecting my accent, most everyone wanted to know more about my personal life: where I was born, when and how I came to the US and about my family.

Norm and his wife, Pauline, and I became very close personal friends. They took me in as if I were their long-lost brother. They, like so many other incredible people, gave me both opportunities and the help and encouragement I needed to succeed along the way.

Two of my most memorable success stories in selling landscaping were to the president and vice president of a huge international packing company out of Palmyra, New York. They both needed landscape plans and lots of shrubs. The job on the first house was so big I asked Norm to help me. It took several days to measure and draw up the plan. The cost of the entire nursery stock was equal to approximately one third the cost of the house. He went for it.

I was on my own with the vice president. He loved the plan but felt it would overextend his budget doing everything at one time. So, for now, he decided to plant grass for his small acreage and complete the project in spring. Still nothing to complain about. The commission I made off the $9,000 worth of grass seed I sold him almost made one car payment.

The president was the one who offered me a job selling their products and services across Europe. There was a time I would have jumped at the chance, but by now I was on my way to establishing a new life and career in sales right here in the good old USA. I actually gave it some thought for a few days; then I respectfully declined his offer and thanked him for the opportunity.

For the remainder of 1956, I continued to build my business. However, by the time wintery weather arrived in upstate New York, no one wanted to talk about rose bushes or landscaping. By the time the new year rolled around, money was getting low, and I sure didn't want to take a chance on losing my beautiful car. It was time to move fast and find something more substantial. One of my friends suggested I contact an employment agency to help search for a sales position. Several opportunities were available, but one was of particular interest to me as it included travel. The Otto Bernz Company right there in Rochester was expanding their operations and was hiring additional promotional sales people to develop new territories throughout the US.

After my discharge from the US Army, I wanted to go into sales at that time, but every job I looked at wanted a person with sales experience and, preferably, a college degree. I had the degree, but I certainly didn't have any sales experience then. Now, I had both. I figure if I can just get my foot in the door for an interview, I'll have a good chance of getting my dream job.

I answered the ad and got an appointment right away with Mr. Waigand, the promotional sales manager. I show up for the meeting both excited and anxious. Mr. Waigand put me at ease right away. He asked me where I was from, how and when I came to the US, you know, the normal questions almost everyone asked me. He was quite surprised when I told him he had the same last name as my mother's family: Waigand. The interview turned out to be more of a personal rather than business nature. At the end of our conversation, he told me they were looking for fifteen exceptional individuals who could help them successfully expand a new sales and marketing program across the US. Then he asked,

"Can you come back for another interview next week? I still have thirty or forty more applicants to look at."

"Yes sir, I can be here."

"Okay, make an appointment with my secretary on your way out. I'll see you next week."

I left the Bernz office excited, very hopeful and optimistic. After all, I already booked my second interview before I even left his office on the first one. Finally, I return for my second interview with Mr. Waigand. He thanked me for coming in and then went straight into detail about the job description and company expectations of new hires. Then he said,

"Now Rudy, let me ask you: What makes you think you can sell our products?"

And before even taking time to think, I blurted out,

"What makes you think I can't?"

"Okay, that settles it. You're hired."

Excited? Oh yes, but there was paperwork to fill out and other personnel matter to attend to. I had to talk to myself,

"Save the excitement for later; right now, it's time to take care of business."

Once all that was done, I was instructed to show up one week later to begin my three-week office and factory training program.

After a week of celebrating my new job with everyone I knew, I arrive almost an hour early my first day at work. Finally, all the new hires meet at the designated office and are welcomed to the company with issuance of our name tags, note pads and other items they wanted us to have. Other staff members came in to meet us. We were made to feel very welcomed and appreciated. After Mr. Waigand finished a short overview presentation of the company product line, we were then escorted into the factory area and introduced to all the factory workers.

That first day was mostly about welcoming us to the company. Introductions and familiarization with products manufactured at the Otto Bernz Company. For the next week, we learned all about the manufacturing process and even worked on the assembly line. After all, it was important to learn all we could about our product line. At the end of the week, we were given a test. So, maybe I hadn't taken this new job quite as seriously as I should have. Partying every night seemed to be more important than studying at the time. To my surprise, I flunked the test by a couple of points. Mr. Waigand brought me in to his office and closed the door and asked me to have a seat. I was so humiliated and disappointed in myself. He just shuffled papers on his desk while I sat there in silence, squirming I'm sure. I thought my head was going to burst wide open. After letting me sweat it out for a few minutes, he looks up, smiles at me and said,

"I'm not sure what happened on the test, Rudy. Maybe you didn't understand the meaning of some of the more technical questions in English, but I have no doubt with just a little time studying this worksheet you can pass this test with no problem at all."

He handed me the worksheets and politely walked me to the door.

"Thank you, Mr. Waigand. I won't let you down. I won't disappoint you."

I was really talking to myself. Were it not for Mr. Waigand believing in me and wanting me to succeed, I may have just made one of the biggest mistakes of my life. Two days later after office hours, Mr. Waigand brought me into his office to retake the test. He did some paperwork while I ran through the test and in no time; I was finished. He went through it quickly, looked up, smiled and said,

"Good job, I never had any doubt. You'll do great with our company. I'll see you bright and early tomorrow morning."

From that day forward, at twenty-six years old, I had no problem placing my priorities. When it's time to party, it's time to party. When it's time to work, then it's time to get down to business.

We were all in field training for the next couple of weeks, calling on local hardware stores until territory assignments were announced. My first assignment was in Missouri and Kansas.

For the next two years, I had the time of my life. My dream job turned out to be everything and more than I could have ever imagined. Within this two-year period, I was on seven-day expense because I ended up traveling not only Missouri and Kansas, but Illinois, Wisconsin, Texas, Louisiana, Indiana, Ohio and Kentucky. How lucky to get paid to see the USA.

In the fall of 1959, I was called to a national sales meeting in Rochester. My boss asked if I'd like to have the Texas/Louisiana territory. Okay with me. I had never been to either state, so it was a chance to see more of the US while on full expense. He asked me to try it and let him know after a certain time how I liked it.

Within three weeks, I phoned and told him this territory was not worth the trouble and expense, certainly compared to the success of the territory I just left. He asked me to hang in for a while longer, promising to fly me back to Rochester for the Christmas party and we'd talk about it then.

Houston was my home base at the time. I continued to see this good-looking little blonde at the same restaurant I ate lunch at quite often. She also played piano and sang in a cozy little piano bar and supper club connected with the same restaurant/hotel owned by Houston oil man, Howard Lee. I saw her in there a few times but never got up the nerve to approach her.

About a week before I left for Rochester, I finally asked the restaurant manager about the good-looking blonde I kept seeing in the restaurant.

"Sure, I know her. She works just across the street. Her name is Kay Lewis. She is a very nice girl and comes from a nice family in southeast Texas. Her father is superintendent of a school near Beaumont. I can probably arrange a meeting if you would like to meet her."

L.V. kept her word, and a couple days later Kay and I met for lunch. We had a great time talking about all sorts of things. I told her I was leaving for Rochester and asked if I could call her when I returned after the holidays.

The Christmas party was a blast. I invited my friends Norm and Pauline. There was plenty to eat and drink. We heard lots of salesmen's stories from all over the country. It was great seeing everyone again.

My boss never asked me about the Texas territory, and I never mentioned it to him again. After all, I had developed somewhat of a special interest in Houston.

Surprises! Surprise! Surprise!
January 1960

A few days after I return to Houston and get my work schedule in order, I phone Kay and ask her out for a dinner date that following Saturday. During the phone conversation, she told me that was her birthday and accepted my invitation. I immediately made dinner reservations at an upscale English restaurant, The Red Lion, specializing in prime rib.

Kay looked beautiful. We had a cocktail at her place then left for dinner. She loved my choice of restaurant. I even ordered dinner for her. I remember exactly what I ordered for both of us: London Grill—their specialty of the house. I excused myself from the table after dinner and told our waiter in private we were celebrating Kay's birthday. He surprised her with a beautiful specialty of the house dessert, candle and all.

It was the perfect date. This was a girl I could talk to. I'm pretty sure by the time I left her place, I had told her my whole life history. I picked her up for brunch the next day and for a date the next night...and the next night, etc., etc. I was on the road quite a lot covering my huge territory of Texas and Louisiana, but we spent every possible moment together when I was in Houston.

Toward the end of April, I went to Memphis for a regional sales meeting and was immediately told I was being transferred back to Rochester for a new assignment. I phoned Kay at work right away and gave her the news.

The next night, she picked me up at the airport, and we stopped in at our favorite little jazz club, Club Gulfgate, for a drink. Our favorite trio was playing, and Kay asked me to dance.

That's when she told me,

"I quit my job and we're getting married."

Silence.

I was so shocked; I really didn't even know how to react to that and finally, I asked,

"We are?"

"Yes, we are. But you have to propose to me first."

"I do?"

The more we talked about it, the more I knew she had made up her mind. At twenty-nine years of age, single, traveling across the country on my own, I had quite a few girlfriends, but never one like this one. Maybe she's just what I needed; someone to make my mind up for me. I had given marriage a thought on occasion, but I guess I hadn't met the right girl yet.

"I'm waiting,' she said.

"Waiting for what?" I replied.

"Waiting for you to propose."

"Okay, how about it?" I asked.

We had a good laugh and enjoyed quite a celebration.

Although happy about the idea of getting married, I was not sure how our lifestyle was going to work out with my job. But Kay was so determined; I knew it would work out somehow. The next day, I called Norm and Pauline to tell them that I was being transferred back to Rochester and that Kay and I were getting married. They were thrilled and, after some discussion over the next couple of days, they insisted we stay with them. I would go on my assignment, and Pauline and Kay would plan the wedding. Done. Just like that.

We went to Kay's parents to explain the situation about my transfer and told them of our plans. I guess back in those days, a "good girl" didn't "run off" and get married for no good reason. They were not happy about us eloping, as it was called back in those days, and were quite suspicious of our sudden plans to marry. Somewhere in the conversation, someone mentioned that "only time will tell." They did not want to accept the actual circumstances and facts of the situation. Kay did not falter. Despite her family's disapproval, we proceeded with our plans to leave together to live our new life.

We made it to Rochester. Kay, Pauline and Norm fell in love with one another. I reported to headquarters and told my boss of my plans to marry. He was not happy at all about that, as the company had big plans for me that didn't include a wife and settling down. I went ahead with company plans, troubleshooting in Michigan for six weeks. Kay and Pauline planned the wedding for August 13, two days after I arrived back from Michigan.

Pauline was catering manager at the beautiful Sheraton Hotel in Rochester. We had a rather small, but beautiful wedding at the Episcopal Church in Rochester with a nice reception at the hotel. It was so great having a gathering of all my friends and former bosses and co-workers there for the wedding and to meet my bride.

We went on a week-long honeymoon in upstate New York in the Adirondack Mountains in the Lake Placid area with a swing through Niagara Falls on the way back.

My sales manager was still totally against my getting married and having a wife now to consider. I convinced him I could be married and still do a good job for the company. Kay and I had a great time traveling around the Midwest on seven-day expense for several months. We considered it an extended honeymoon; practically all expenses paid. My next assignment was Illinois and Wisconsin. We packed whatever we could get in our car and left for Chicago, moving into a high rise efficiency apartment on the north shore of Lake Michigan.

For the next several months, I was gone sometimes for two weeks at a time. Kay went to work for Manpower, a temporary employment agency. She landed a great job right away as administrative assistant to the Dean of the dental school at Loyola University in downtown Chicago. This job lasted about four months, and then she went to work for Encyclopedia Britannica in the suburbs of Chicago. This was quite an experience for Kay. She loved it, and it kept her occupied while I was working out of state. In early spring, we bought a sailboat with a mooring right downtown Chicago. We spent every minute of leisure time together either sailing on Lake Michigan or at the beach.

In March, Kay got pregnant, which added a whole other dynamic to my job and to our future. Inevitable change was on the way. We were just not sure what that change would be. The National Housewares Show was held every July and January in Chicago (at the Navy Pier at that time). We visited the show mostly out of curiosity to see what was going on in that industry. We were both tired of my being gone so much of the time and now, with a baby on the way, we kicked around the idea of going into business for ourselves as manufacturer's representatives. We were tired of other people controlling our time and life.

A decision would have to be made soon.

CHAPTER 9

It's All About Timing

■ ■ ■

CHICAGO, JUNE 1961

I WAS CALLED BACK TO the home office for a meeting in Rochester and informed that company cutbacks were on the way. The timing was perfect. I told my sales manager that we were now expecting a baby in December and that we had already made plans to go into the manufacturer's representative business for ourselves in Texas. The timing couldn't have been more perfect.

I called Kay to let her know what was going on. She was the happiest girl alive.

My resignation was announced. Everyone was very happy for us about the baby as well as the decision we made to go into business for ourselves. I got a very nice sendoff, along with letters of recommendation that followed from the president of the company on down.

I flew back to Chicago as an independent agent, free to escalate living the American dream to a whole new level.

Kay and I attended the National Housewares Show in Chicago in July to see what lines we might be able to pick up for the Texas-Oklahoma territory. Every manufacturer I approached asked the same questions,

"How long have you been in business, and what experience do you have as a manufacturer's representative?"

We were happy to take any line anyone was willing to give us as we were starry eyed, eager and ready to be our own boss, schedule our own time and yes, make our millions! We packed up and headed for Dallas. Living in the north, our car didn't have air conditioning. When we arrived, we got the shock of our life. The temperature was 103 degrees Fahrenheit. Welcome to Texas! We spent the first couple of weeks with Kay's Aunt Glenn and Uncle Pete and family in the Dallas area, just long enough to find our own apartment.

We had what we thought would be ample savings to carry us through until the business got rolling. But those *premium* lines we picked up in Chicago were not exactly working out that great. Also, those were the days before computers and inventory control (no, it was not the Dark Ages—only the early '60s). Reps then traveled to each small store with sample bags in hand, showed our "samples" to the buyer and hopefully wrote an order. How much could one small "mom and pop" store purchase? I kept plugging away with little results. We kept thinking that if we could just hold out until we got that big break or that great line of items everyone wanted, we'd be okay. To say we economized or lived conservatively is a total understatement. We had a doctor to pay and, by the time we paid rent, business travel expenses, food and absolute necessities, our savings were dwindling fast. It was all going out with very little coming in. "Underfunded" also took on a whole new meaning. We knew somehow, at some point, if we could just hang on, things would turn around. We just didn't know how or when.

Things were looking pretty bleak on the financial front, but the excitement about our new baby outweighed all other worries at the moment. On December 23, 1961, our baby girl Katherine Ann was born. That was also Uncle Pete's birthday. Pete and Glen spent the whole day at the hospital with me. Kay was in labor for fourteen hours.

On Christmas day, I pick up Kay and Ann from the hospital. To let you know just how bad things were, we had less than $30 in the bank and a few dollars in our pocket. The next day, Pete and Glen pay us a surprise visit; each of them carrying two big sacks of groceries. They claimed they just wanted to cook for us since we just had the baby. It was a real party. We forgot that we were almost dead broke. After all the sacks were emptied, our small cupboard was completely filled with flour, sugar, box foods, pasta and canned goods plus a few packages of meat for our freezer. We only had two dozen diapers (the old fashioned kind that get laundered) and three or four little gowns Kay made by hand from small pieces of material she bought at the variety store.

After we ate, Pete went to the car and brought in another big sack filled to the top with something. He emptied the sack onto our bed and, to our total surprise, they had brought two dozen diapers, complete "layette" (gowns and little shirts, etc), sox and booties, a little jacket, a couple of little newborn ru fru dresses, blankets, and a number of toiletry items needed for a new baby. I was appreciative, but Kay, in particular, was so happy and thankful. They were definitely our angels looking after us.

In early January, we received a decent commission check that got us through for the next couple of months.

Meanwhile, through friends of ours at the apartment, we met Nancy and Chuck Richter and their daughter, Vivian, who just moved to Dallas from Los Angeles. We took an instant liking to each other. They absolutely fell in love with our baby, Ann. They were just like family. Chuck grew up in Milwaukee, Wisconsin, of German descent. We had many things in common. His family lived through the depression in the US, and my family and I lived through the war in Europe. We shared many stories about our history. It felt as though we were brothers. We became each other's adopted family and had lots of great times together.

Chuck was in management with a leading national brokerage firm and had been transferred to Dallas. They lived in a beautiful four-bedroom house in the suburbs. We visited, ate and played cards with them almost every weekend.

Meanwhile, Kay took a job in downtown Dallas as administrative assistant to the Executive of Boy Scouts of America. She was heartbroken to leave Ann with a babysitter, but without the extra salary, we were finished. Even with Kay's salary, we were barely hanging on. We just knew that every new line we picked up was going to be the "next big thing," but somehow, so far, it had not worked out that way. If only we could hold on until we got our first big break.

Nan and Chuck were well aware of our struggles and sacrifice along with our determination to make this work. Out of the blue one night during a card game, Chuck told us they wanted to talk with us about something. He proceeded to tell us that he and Nan had talked it over, and they would like for us to come stay with them for a few months until we got on our feet; that Nan would keep Ann while Kay worked every day, and we could contribute to the grocery bill when we could. We were totally floored and couldn't imagine such an offer, but they said it was already settled. We'd move after we gave notice at our apartment.

Business was hard to come by. We just didn't have the lines we needed to build any sales volume and, although I had a lot of sales experience, I was new in this particular line of business and had not had time to build a rapport with the buyers. It was hard to break through. I was constantly looking for new lines, and several of my rep friends were also trying to hook me up with manufacturers they knew.

Computer ordering systems with inventory control took hold in this industry in the early '60s and we were right there to benefit from such a new innovation.

As luck and determination would have it, I began to get the attention of several importers. I was actually offered a couple of really nice lines that already had some volume built in the territory, and things started to pop. We began to sell to the grocery chains first; then went on to variety chain stores. The more chain stores we sold to, the better lines we were able to acquire. Instead of selling items to one small mom and pop store, we were now selling to one buyer at a central location that distributed to 50-60-70-100 stores. We began to receive order confirmation printouts in the mail in large envelopes and, sometimes, in boxes.

This was in the early days of the Gibson Discount Centers chain stores with buying offices in Seagoville, just outside Dallas. We participated in the first Gibson trade show in 1962, held at the old Baker Hotel in downtown Dallas. (of Jack Ruby fame). By that time, we were selling all kinds of houseware products. In fact, we were getting the reputation of "the kitchen gadget kings." Everyone knew Seamayer Sales was responsible for a very big percentage of kitchen gadgets going into all these chain stores. We sold kitchen gadgets by the hundreds of gross to chain stores. There were well over a hundred items in the line, and it continued to grow.

Thanks to Chuck and Nancy for providing the bridge that took us from near collapse to the beginning of an incredibly successful manufacturer's representative business that lasted for thirty-five years.

We moved from Nan's and Chuck's into our very own new three-bedroom, two-bath brick house (with wood shingles that were optional at $100 extra). Man, we were living now! It was such a joyous time. And to think how quickly things turned around once we got rolling. Our determination, along with Nan's and Chuck's help, began to pay off in ways we couldn't have even imagined.

Ann was five and five and a half years old when we had our next baby girl, Karen, and then along comes Erika a couple of years later.

Kay and I were great life and business partners. Our office was in our home for many years. She wore many hats. I was on the road a lot selling while she was home running the office, taking care of our three girls, Ann, Karen and Erika, the dogs and cats, the house, and anything else that needed care. She was a great cook and an excellent seamstress. She made all our girls' clothing for years. I never had to worry about the home front when I was on the road. I knew she was there; strong, taking care of everyone and doing what needed to be done in the office. We worked all the trade shows together. Not many women/wives were involved directly or indirectly for that matter, in the rep business with their husbands in those days, but I relied and depended upon her. She was definitely respected and was an integral part of the success we enjoyed. She always said, when it came to business, she was "just one of the guys." Well, not exactly; she didn't look like any guy I knew, but she was smart in business and had a nice way of dealing with customers, manufacturers and shippers. She could do it all, including keeping me in line (most of the time).

In the early '70s, we picked up the Sauder Woodworking/Foremost Furniture line manufactured in Archbold, Ohio. This was in the early days of "ready to assemble" or furniture in a box. The *do it yourself take home and assemble* concept really caught on. It was extremely affordable, and the quality and product line continued to improve and grow. We sold to one chain store after another until we were into all the major chain stores in Texas and Oklahoma.

The massive Dallas World Trade Center, which was part of the Trammel Crow Market Center project, opened in 1974. The timing was perfect. Anyone who was "anyone" in the wholesale business now had permanent showrooms and offices in either the Apparel Mart or the new World Trade Center. The World Trade Center opened with seven floors.

Before the carpet was even laid on the top floor, we were under contract and having the time of our life decorating our own showroom. Kay and I both were *living* our own American Dream…together. It was a great time for us and for our children in so many ways.

The furniture line grew to the point that we took a showroom on the fifth floor several times the size of our first little showroom. Our import lines were primarily from Austria and Germany, which gave us more opportunities to travel to Europe for business and pleasure; sometimes, bringing our daughters along. The US dollar was strong during much of this time. On occasion, we ordered new cars from the Mercedes factory in Sindelfingen, Germany, to drive on vacations then ship back home for our use here.

We were not without personal and business challenges from time to time, but that's just life. We made it through the tough times with help of others who cared about us and built a business and life we were very proud of. Anyone can live the *American Dream* if that's what they are determined to do. There will always be people there to help. That's what we do in my country, America.

Kay and Rudy's wedding, August 13, 1960

Kay and Rudy
German Day at the State Fair of Texas

Kay and Rudy at Kuby's
German Restaurant, Dallas

Ann, Erika and Karen Seamayer

Rudy and Kay with Erika, Karen and Ann

Erika, Karen and Ann

Living the American Dream

Seamayer Family – Ann, Erika, Kay, Rudy and Karen

Grands – Erika Laine, Nicholas and Alex

Grands – Erika Laine Shockley and Alex Ross

Grand – Nicholas Ross

Rudy and Ann sailing off Long Island, New York

Karen and Rudy

Erika and Rudy

Erika and Erik Williamson

Ross Family – Alex, Darrin, Nicholas and Karen

Kay and Rudy with Grands -
Erika Laine, Nicholas and Alex

CHAPTER 10

Return to My Homeland – 60 Years Later
(Previously Werschetz, Banat Yugoslavia – Now Vrsac, Serbia)

■ ■ ■

"Don't Go Back"
September, 2004

THROUGH THE YEARS, CHILDHOOD FRIENDS and relatives living in Europe who revisited our hometown and surrounding area always discouraged me from going back. The message from each of them was both strong and similar in nature:

"Don't go back. You will be heartbroken to see the unbelievable devastation and decay of our town and the entire region caused by the ravages of war and Communist rule under Marshal Tito."

I never doubted their word or concerns, but the same strong desire that drew all of them back still remained deep in my heart and soul. After all, when we escaped on *The Last Train Out,* October 1, 1944, the plan was to transport all us kids to a safer environment then bring us back home after the war was over. Unfortunately, after the war, the country we once knew no longer existed; we had no country to return to. Those of us who escaped were now displaced persons or persons without a country.

Once Russia captured Yugoslavia, Serbian leader Marshal Tito came to power. Thousands of Germans were captured and were shot or died in Tito's Communist concentration camps.

And now, almost sixty years to the month after my escape in 1944, the time has come to return to my homeland to see for myself. The name of the town has been changed to Vrsac, and the country is now Serbia. Yugoslavia was dissolved in 2003.

A close friend of mine in the Dallas area, Ludwig Kenniger, a famous master wood and stone carver and teacher, originally from Bavaria, agrees to make the trip with me. We fly in to Munich, rent a car and drive to the beautiful little town of Tiefenbach, near Passau on the Danube where Ludwig's nephew Josef and his wife, Anna, live. We have a nice restful visit with Josef and Anna for a couple of days; then the four of us head for Werschetz. Josef graciously agreed to drive us in his car as car rental companies do not allow their vehicles to cross the border into Serbia due to widespread vandalism and thievery. It's good to have them along.

I am both excited *and* anxious to finally return to my birthplace after so many years. The closer we get to the Hungarian/Serbian border, the more anxious I become. After all that time, and after so much has happened, I can't keep from wondering what I will see. How will I feel? Can things really be as bad as reported?

When we arrive at the border, Josef and Anna realize they forgot to bring their passports. This means we either turn back or Ludwig and I continue on in Josef's car without them. After some discussion, we decide to all check into a hotel and stay together that night. Ludwig and I would continue on our journey the next morning. We'd pick up Josef and Anna on our return a couple of days later.

Ludwig and I get an early start the next morning. We cross the border into Serbia and are on our way. However, road conditions are terrible and, to make driving even more difficult, the few road signs still standing are not legible. I would venture to say little to no road repair had been done since the war. We literally guess our way through the whole trip. The drive was both nerve wracking and a bit scary.

Uncertain if we are on the right road to Werschetz after traveling several hours, in the distance I finally see a familiar sight. It's the unforgettable iconic landmark castle on the mountaintop just above our city. What a relief. We're almost there.

The railroad station is our first stop upon arrival in Werschetz. We sit silently for quite some time in the car. As I stare at the station, a feeling of overwhelming sadness and loneliness comes over me as memory takes me to *that* day in October, 1943, hanging out of the train window, waving goodbye to my mother as she follows alongside the train waving back. I close my eyes and see her standing there so clearly it feels as though I can reach out and touch her face. I can't really express how I felt at that moment. After a few seconds, her vision fades just as it did the day we pulled farther and farther from the station on The Last Train Out. I've wondered so many times how things would have been if my mother had left with us on the train that day. The thought of what might have happened to her at the hands of the Russians after the invasion is a horrifying thought.

Ludwig and I sit and talk quietly for a while. It's really good having him along as we both experienced challenges of escape and survival during the war. His understanding of the importance of my return is somehow deeply comforting.

From the rail station, we make our way to the house I lived in. Through the years, I often imagined how I would feel standing at the front door or maybe even taking a look inside.

Most homes then were built with a high concrete type wall around them with double gates that allowed entry into the courtyard either in front or back of the house. Our house was painted bright yellow and trimmed in white. The house across the street from us, with its beautiful gold-painted dome (like a crown) at the entry, was nothing less than a showcase. Our whole street and neighborhood was filled with beautifully kept homes with manicured landscaping; a testament to the hard-working Germans who cared and provided for their families and took pride in their possessions.

As we turn and drive down the street toward my house, it takes no time to fully understand the reasons for all the warnings I got from family and friends about returning. Where once stood beautiful homes now are but overgrown junk piles of rubbish and dilapidated houses. We pull up in front of my house and park across the street. From what we observed on the way, I'm surprised it is still standing. Half of the courtyard wall has fallen down and, from what I can see of the house, it too is in total disrepair. In looking a bit closer, Ludwig and I spot a few patches of very old-looking faded brown paint barely visible on both the house and wall. It's hard to believe, but the house actually appears to be inhabited. From what I see, I have absolutely no desire to even step foot on the property, much less go inside. I'll rely on my childhood memories.

The once-beautiful dome on the house across the street is now streaked and rusty and in general ill repair. I've seen enough.

As we drive through town toward our hotel, we see buildings boarded up, one after another. There are few signs of life other than someone passing by in a horse and buggy or riding on an old bicycle, motorcycle or junker-rattletrap car—most likely put together with leftover parts from the war and held together with wire. There is no evidence of new paint on anything, anywhere.

It is truly devastating to see and even more impossible to believe the doom and gloom that still exists in my town and the country as a result of war, Tito's hell and Milosevic's Communist rule.

We make our way to the city square and locate Hotel Serpid where we have reservations. The hotel clerk is a rather interesting small little dark-haired Serbian fellow wearing a bright red cloth type hat that leans to one side, with a matching red scarf loosely stuffed into the pocket of his wrinkled shirt. I'm rather amused by his interesting hotel clerk uniform.

Although the majority of the town was German-speaking when I lived there, we all learned to speak enough Serbian to protect ourselves from bullies living across town, always ready to pick a fight. Surprisingly, it served me good enough to get us checked into the hotel without any problem.

Up one flight of stairs, we find our room, drop our bags and freshen up a bit. After a long day, we're well overdue for a beer and something to eat. We inquire with the hotel clerk. He directs us to the hotel restaurant down a dimly lighted hallway. With a bit of caution, we proceed toward the door and enter into a very small, rather depressing-looking room with no windows. Three or four small tables with very straight high-backed chairs sit idle. So far, we've not seen any other guests in the hotel. We stand just inside the door and wait a couple minutes. No one shows up, so we choose a table and sit down.

Just then, from behind a beaded curtain in the corner of the room, a waiter appears. We waste no time ordering a local beer. The waiter is a friendly sort of fellow, and between speaking Serbian, English and German he *highly* suggests we order the *house special*, a sampling of their house and regional favorites. Actually, we were not offered any other choices. We figured out later the "house special" was most likely food already cooked and sitting on the stove when we arrived. The beer was really refreshing and, although we were not exactly sure of everything we were eating, we cleaned our plates and could have probably eaten more. They didn't have any deserts cooked, so we had another beer.

We engage in small talk with our waiter and learn that he is of German/Hungarian descent. I recall the name of Zopfman Brewery and ask if he can tell me what happened to it. He was surprised I knew or remembered this name. My question paved the way for quite an open conversation between us.

"Well, obviously, you've known this region for quite a long time. So what brings you to Werschetz; and why now? " the waiter asked.

"I am of German descent, was born here and fled sixty years ago at age fourteen, just hours before the Russians moved in. I've put off coming back for many reasons, but at this point in my life, it is important that I revisit my homeland and my childhood. There are many questions that have never been answered. I'm not sure I'll get any answers now, but I had to return to see with my own eyes what others have told me about on past visits here. It is a very sad past for me and my family and friends and the country I once called *home*."

He began telling Ludwig and me stories he said he had heard all his life from family about life during and after the war.

"It is well known and documented that after WWII; the Communists confiscated all the German breweries, businesses, homes and personal property and redistributed them to "Party" members in power. The very few Germans who escaped had a difficult time reaching Austria or Germany. Some made it across into Romania and Hungary only to be shot in the back after negotiating their crossing with bribes of jewelry and money. Many German men who remained were shot at night in large groups with machine guns. The women were ordered to load the bodies onto horse-drawn wagons to be taken outside the city and dumped into mass graves."

There was silence for several seconds, and then he asked me if I'd tell him what I knew about those times.

After going to the train station, my house and all through the town, many memories, long forgotten, had been refreshed by it all. I wondered if staying at this hotel, eating at this hotel restaurant, with this particular waiter serving us was coincidental in any way. Whatever the case, he had a good understanding of some of the regional history and politics of those times and seemed to have a genuine interest in learning more.

"I've heard similar stories through the years. Sometime in 1948 in Germany, I met a lady from Werschetz who, along with her three daughters, escaped from one of Tito's Communist death camps. She claimed to have met and known my mother for a short time inside the same camp she and her daughters were in and was positive she died of sickness and starvation within three weeks after her capture; but of course, we have no proof of her story.

"The lady went on to tell us that Tito had but one purpose in mind; to root out all the Germans from Yugoslavia. On a daily basis, Germans were driven from their homes, shot on site or marched to the nearest death camp. The older or weak ones who could not keep up were shot on the way. Women and young girls were raped and families robbed of anything of value. When a German shot a Russian or Communist partisan soldier trying to protect themselves or during or after a rape or murder, he would be shot by a mob of partisan soldiers in the street with machine guns. Catholic priests were brutally beaten and killed, and churches were robbed of all their holy artifacts. The German people lived daily with this indescribable fear and uncertainty.

"My cousin Ferdinand got shot on the Romanian border trying to escape. My cousin Tilde survived four years in one of the Russian work camps in Siberia. Another one of my mother's brothers, Ignatz, and his wife, Frieda, and their two young children escaped safely across the border into Romania, only to be captured and held for twenty years working as slaves in commercial vegetable fields. They were finally released in the mid-1960s with the clothes on their backs and ended up in southern Germany, near Salzburg. It was a horrible existence for them. The German government paid them reparations for their losses during WWII in Yugoslavia as they too were of German descent. Thankfully, they built a nice house and lived a peaceful life for many years.

"In 1947, a good number of Germans still remained in Yugoslavia, living under Communist rule. Unlike Hitler and his desire to annihilate all the Jews, Tito realized he could not kill all the Germans in Yugoslavia. They had already been robbed of their wealth, food was scarce and it was reported (many times by those who lived through it) that Tito simply opened the borders and ordered them to leave the country. By the time this massive evacuation was over in 1948, some 40,000 Germans fled across the border into Hungary and close to 100,000 ended up in Germany.

"Tito and his bandits managed to destroy, in a very short time, what took the industrious hard-working disciplined Germans over 200 years to build.

"I have personal accounts of some of the townspeople revisiting our city in the 1950s and '60s only to find confusion and chaos. It was sadly reported that our Catholic cemetery was completely leveled, and apartment buildings were erected. For some strange reason, the cemetery chapel was left untouched. A childhood friend of mine who now lives in Vienna visited our town and took photos. He, along with others, advised me never to return—ever again."

We finally end our conversation with the waiter, thank him for taking the time to visit with us, and then pay our bill. After our long and stressful day and a hearty and satisfying meal along with a couple of beers, Ludwig and I are all too happy to turn in early.

Day Two in Werschetz

I didn't sleep much last night, but nonetheless, it's time to get up and be on our way. After breakfast and checkout, Ludwig and I visit the twin tower Neogothic Saint Gerard Catholic Church, which was built between 1860 and 1863. It is as beautiful as ever, and from what we've seen in the city so far, it's an incredibly welcoming and comforting sight. It surely must have been divine intervention that saved this church as so many others were destroyed throughout Europe during the war.

On one of my reunion visits back to Lake Chimsee in Bavaria, I learned that our church had been kept in good repair and fully operational throughout the post war years from generous donations of Germans who once lived and attended church there.

After spending time in the church, we drive back by the train station and other landmarks in town, take some pictures and begin our journey back to pick up Josef and Anna in Hungary.

Our return trip was just as stressful as the one coming down to Werschetz. Highway signs were just as bad going north as they were coming south. We got lost a few times.

The majority of the rattletrap cars we saw were Jugos built at one time in Yugoslavia by Fiat of Italy. I would guess car owners stole parts from one another to keep their vehicles running.

All my friends were right. It's almost impossible to believe what happened to our town; to our country. I thank God every day for my freedom and for the great life I have in America with my family.

Communist rule in Serbia killed the goose that laid the golden egg during the war when they destroyed the industrious, hard-working successful German population. Serbia is a total disaster from everything I saw. The country has digressed at least one hundred years since then.

Overcast skies and light rain speak for my level of sadness as I say a final goodbye to my homeland and to the memory of my mother. I totally understand now why everyone advised me to stay away. But, just like all of them, I had to see, know and feel it all for myself. It is just something that had to be done, no matter how painful.

Return from Hell

By the time we reach the toll road, we are starving and begin to look for a place to eat. We notice a few cars ahead of us taking a certain exit. We follow behind them in hopes they too are hungry. After driving a few blocks through a small community, we end up in a parking lot with one way in and one way out, which is a bit alarming to us.

We get out of the car. Ludwig asked with a half grin,

"How did we get here?"

"You are the co-pilot. You tell me," I answered, as we begin to laugh at the situation and ourselves.

Just then, a nicely dressed lady about to get in her car in the same parking lot spotted our license plate from Germany. She sensed we were lost from overhearing our conversation and came over to offer her help. She spoke good English. I told her that we were looking for someplace to eat. She smiled and said,

"See that red car over there? Just follow me. I'll take you to a nice restaurant."

We follow her and end up in another small parking lot, but there's no restaurant in site. Rather anxious at this moment, we got out of the car gesturing to the lady as if to say "where is the restaurant? We don't see any restaurant."

I was beginning to think we might be set up for either a robbery or a carjacking, or both. After all, we are still in Serbia. She gets out of her car and points as she speaks,

"We can't drive over there; we'll have to walk about a hundred yards to the restaurant."

Now I'm really suspicious and worried that we are being led away from Josef's and Anna's beautiful black Mercedes; a sort of diversionary action to make it easy on robbers to steal the car. After all, this sort of thing goes on all over the former eastern bloc; good reason car rental companies will not allow their cars to be driven into these areas.

She walks over to us, introduces herself and insists on walking us to the restaurant. She even walks inside and tells the manager she has brought him two new customers. She was very personable and quick to help us. We invite her for a glass of wine. She thanks us but declines, explaining she was on her way to meet up with her daughter when she saw us in the dead-end parking lot.

Ludwig and I were seated at a table with hideous King Arthur type chairs. The arms of the chairs reached our armpits. The waiter comes over and gives us a menu. We both decided on the Hungarian goulash. After all, what could go wrong? We were in an area of Serbia that once belonged to Hungary. I'll just say the bread and butter and wine were very good and filled the gap. Thank goodness our earlier worries were unwarranted. Josef's car was sitting right where we left it, and soon we were on our way.

Once back on the tollway headed north, I put the pedal to the metal. We wanted to make it across the Serbian-Hungarian border to Zagreb by around three o'clock, if possible, to pick up Josef and Anna. We make good time and drive around the town for about twenty minutes looking for the hotel. Lost again. I was so stressed out driving, all I could think about was finding them and turning the keys over to Josef. And now, we can't even find the hotel! Just as we turned down another one-way street, we hear Josef call out,

"Rudy, Ludwig, over here; we're over here."

I slam on the breaks and bring the car to a screeching halt. We look around, and there they are sitting at a sidewalk café having a beer. Josef just happened to spot his car. I immediately pull over to the side of the street and wait for them to pay their check and meet us. I was never so glad to just ride. Josef drove to the hotel, picked up their bags, loaded up and we were off to Budapest. Naturally, they wanted to know all about our trip. Ludwig and I obliged all the way to Budapest.

Upon arrival, we checked into a bed and breakfast. Since none of us knew the city, we ordered a taxi and asked him to take us to a typical Hungarian restaurant. As we begin to relax with a good bottle of wine, listening to a small band play some hot Hungarian and Russian music, Anna, who is of German descent from Russia, begins to dance and twirl just like a professional. It was a good time to just relax, have fun and enjoy all being together.

We arrived back at our place around midnight. Ludwig and I took a quick shower, and off to bed we went.

We wake up around six o'clock and begin to prepare to leave on our journey back to Tiefenbach.

"Ludwig, did you see my watch and ring? I'm positive I left it right here on the nightstand last night before I took my shower."

"No," Ludwig answers. "I haven't seen them."

We all but tore that room up looking for my jewelry until we finally accepted that they must have been stolen during the night. There were no locks on the door, so the night before we pulled the nightstand slightly in front of the door to keep it closed.

We had the owners call the police. When they arrived, we got nowhere with them. They were of no help at all. It was finally suggested that we follow them to the police station to make out a formal report. We wait an hour for some individual to show up who speaks both English and German. He shows. We make the report. He gives me a copy. It's all written in Hungarian. I couldn't resist asking,

"What are the chances of ever getting my jewelry back? "

He lays both hands on the counter, leans over to get closer as if he's going to tell me a secret, looks straight at me and answers in a quiet, almost apologetic voice,

"Zero."

Well, I just *had* to ask.

Finally, we're on our way again. We were all glad to cross the border into Austria and then into Germany; into safety and cleanliness surrounded by a vibrant world of convenience, life and living.

The remaining few days of our trip in Germany visiting friends were pleasant enough but now, particularly after my sad and disturbing experience in Serbia, I'm lonesome to embrace my family.

I've never been so proud to be an American - and I can't wait to get back *home* where I belong.

Werschetz, Yugoslavia

Rudy sailing in the
New York Harbor

Statue of Liberty

Made in the USA
San Bernardino, CA
17 December 2015